Bicycling Through Civil War History

D1567809

Bicycling Through Civil War History

in Maryland, West Virginia, Pennsylvania and Virginia

Kurt B. Detwiler

EPM Publications, Inc.
McLean, Virginia

Library of Congress Cataloging-in-Publication Data

Detwiler, Kurt B.
    Bicycling Through Civil War history: a guide to the
Mid-Atlantic / Kurt B. Detwiler.
        p. cm.
    Includes index.
    ISBN 0-939009-82-X
    1. Maryland—History—Civil War, 1861–1865—
Battlefields— Guildebooks. 2. Virginia—History—Civil War,
1861–1865—Battlefields—Guidebooks. 3. West Virginia—
History—Civil War, 1861–1865—Battlefields—Guidebooks. 4.
Pennsylvania—History—Civil War, 1861–1865—Battlefields—
Guidebooks. 5. United States—History—Civil War, 1861–1865—
Battlefields—Guidebooks. 6. Bicycle touring—Maryland—
Guidebooks. 7. Bicycle touring—Virginia—Guidebooks. 8. Bicycle
touring—West Virginia—guidebooks. 9. Bicycle touring—
Pennsylvania—Guidebooks. 10. Middle Atlantic States—
Guidebooks. I. Title
    E470.2.D47 1994
    917.504'43—dc20   94-33227
                                                                       CIP

Copyright © 1994 Kurt B. Detwiler
All Rights Reserved
EPM Publications, Inc., 1003 Turkey Road
    McLean, VA 22101
Printed in the United States of America

Design: Michael Konetzka/Garruba Dennis Design

Cover photograph of Antietam National Battlefield
by Peter Heimlicher

All black and white photography by Kurt Detwiler

Contents

to Jennifer

Acknowledgments

I wish to express my appreciation to the many people and organizations that assisted in this project. Much of the research and bicycling involved was conducted at National Parks. Without exception, I found National Park employees and volunteers considerate and energized by their important mission. They always had time for my, sometimes obscure, questions and contributed many useful suggestions.

Many Visitor Centers, historical societies and advocacy groups were also invaluable with this research. These include the Montgomery County, MD Historical Society, the Westminster, MD Visitor Center, the Frederick, MD Visitor Center, the Winchester, VA Visitor Center, the Culpeper, VA Chamber of Commerce, the Fredericksburg, VA Visitor Center, the Williamsburg, VA Visitor Center, the Civil War Trust, and the Association for the Preservation of Civil War Sites. Both the Poolesville, MD and the Brunswick, MD public libraries helped in the acquisition of certain hard to find sources.

Special thanks to Jennifer Batchelder, Peter Heimlicher, Ben Smith, Mark Stephens, Matt Andrews, Chris Calkins, Bob Leftwich, Vicki Russell, and Sprigg Lynn.

Finally, this book exists because of the encouragement and kind attention of Evelyn Metzger and the staff of EPM Publications, Inc.

Map List

Maryland

1. John Brown's Farm, *18*
2. South Mountain, *24*
3. Antietam: Ride A, *32*
   Antietam: Ride B, *38*
4. Frederick, *42*
5. Sugarloaf Mountain, *49*
6. Poolesville, *55*
7. Carroll County, *62*
8. Fort Washington-
   Fort Foote, *68*
9. John Wilkes Booth's
   Ride, *72*

West Virginia

10. Harpers Ferry, *78*
11. Shepherdstown, *83*

Pennsylvania

12. Gettysburg: Ride A, *89*
    Gettysburg: Ride B, *96*
    Gettysburg: Ride C, *101*

Virginia

13. Winchester, *107*
    Winchester: Detail, *108*
14. Strasburg: Ride A, *115*
    Strasburg: Ride B, *120*
15. Port Republic, *124*
16. Middleburg, *132*
17. Culpeper, *139*
18. Fredericksburg, *145*
19. Chancellorsville-
    Wilderness, *151*
20. Spotsylvania, *158*
21. Williamsburg-Yorktown, *165*
22. Malvern Hill-Glendale, *172*
23. Fort Harrison, *179*
24. Petersburg, *185*
25. Sayler's Creek, *192*

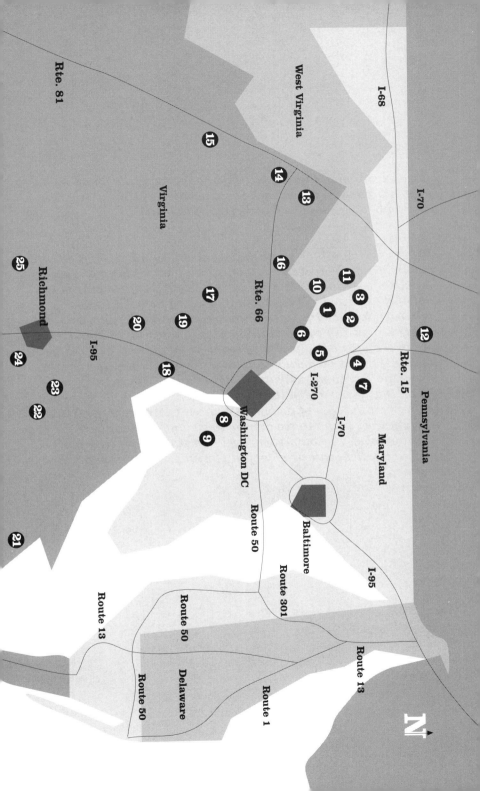

It was surprising that Nature had gone tranquilly on with her golden process in the midst of so much devilment.

Stephen Crane, *The Red Badge of Courage*

It calls first of all for an attitude, a frame of mind, a brooding awareness of the tragedy that once befell our country and an honest attempt to understand the far-reaching results which grew out of that tragedy. It calls upon us to be fully adult in our approach to it, so that we can make ourselves familiar with the hot passions and human blindnesses that led up to it and grew out of it and can realize that greatness went hand in hand with meanness, that men caught up in a tide too strong for them to resist did somehow accomplish more than they meant to accomplish, that the whole of the terrible process did in the end mean more than the sum of its parts. We need to realize that although we are never going to reach a complete understanding of the war, it is not wholly incomprehensible; that it was infinitely more than a needless catastrophe, full of sound and fury, signifying nothing.

Bruce Catton, *Lest We Forget...*

Introduction

The public's fascination with the American Civil War has not waned in the years since Robert E. Lee's surrender at Appomattox Court House. One of the most important manifestations of this fascination has been the conservancy movement. Americans have focused their attention on Civil War preservation more than on any aspect of our rich national heritage. Efforts began with the creation of the first five Civil War Military Parks in the 1890s and continued with the struggle to save the Brandy Station Battlefield, the Cedar Creek Battlefield and dozens of other lesser known sites. While this effort has been conducted through many different organizations, including national and state agencies and private and public trusts, all efforts have been united by a common ideal. This uniting ideal is that the preservation of these sites is integral to our understanding of one of America's most important historical events.

We have sensed as a nation that to truly comprehend the vast struggle that consumed this previous generation, we must not only read about it, but we must also preserve and visit the fields, woods and buildings where this struggle took place. Of course, by visiting these sites one is able to achieve a better understanding of geographic features that affected the war and specific army logistics. However, the real importance may be the sense of spirit that pervades these hauntingly beautiful places. This is a spirit of both event and place that I believe allows the visitor the opportunity for true insightful reflection. And it is this reflection that leads not only to an understanding of the Civil War, but to an understanding of our own continuing struggles and perhaps to a better life for our descendants.

Each year, millions of people do visit these Civil War sites. Thousands of these people enhance their visits by using their bicycles to tour battlefields, small towns and lightly traveled country roads. They have discovered that the bicycle is the finest method of transportation for these regions. Bicyclists are able to read interpretive markers and view battlefields without the inconvenience of parking an automobile. Bicyclists can also acquire a better feel for the geography that dictated much of the war. Bicyclists get an enjoyable workout, moving over some of

America's most scenic terrain at a pace much more in harmony with the Civil War. Finally, the bicycle is quiet, non-polluting and less obtrusive than the automobile in these serene landscapes.

However, until now, there has been no Civil War guidebook for bicyclists. Bicyclists have had to rely on their own exploration and the few automobile guides available from the National Park Service. This guidebook has been researched and written for the Civil War enthusiast and recreational bicyclist. Routes have been chosen for their historical significance, scenic beauty, safety and convenience. I have varied the length and terrain of these rides to make them enjoyable for bicyclists of all skill levels. Bicyclists with more experience can easily combine rides with common starting points to make longer, more challenging rides. Novice riders can start with the many easy rides and work their way up to those requiring more stamina.

Each section contains detailed ride instructions, a ride map and brief historical narrative. A reading selection for further exploration has been included. Also included in most sections are hiking suggestions and details. (Hiking is another great way to explore Civil War history.) All starting points are located within a three-hour drive of Washington, D.C. Complete directions to safe public parking are included.

During the last decade, I have bicycled over 90,000 miles throughout the United States. None of this bicycling has been any more pleasurable than the riding I've done in compiling this guide. The varied terrain, excellent road surfaces, moderate climate, scenic beauty and historical richness all contribute to the pleasure of these rides. I hope you enjoy them as well. I also hope the rides contribute to your understanding of the Civil War, the importance of historical preservation and the continuing shared responsibility of perfecting ideals of equal citizenship for all Americans.

Bicycling

Bicycling is a safe activity. By paying attention to equipment and following a few simple rules, the chance of physical injury or discomfort can be almost completely eliminated. In addition to the following suggestions, it is essential to establish a rapport with your local bicycle professional. Besides being the source of quality equipment and service, bicycle shops serve as an important source of information for the bicycling community. They often conduct mechanical and riding seminars and sponsor rides. They can also recommend a local bicycling club that will match your level and personality.

Bicycles

Of course, the most critical piece of bicycling equipment is the bicycle. There are hundreds of manufacturers and thousands of models, though there are just three basic styles of adult bicycles, each with its own distinct characteristics. Rely on your local bicycle professional for help in choosing the proper style and correct size for you.

The road bicycle is lightweight and has drop handlebars, narrow tires and at least twelve gears. (Sorry, the ten speed is a thing of the past.) It is designed for paved roads, although it can also be used on hard packed dirt trails. Road bicycles handle quickly and climb efficiently.

The mountain bicycle has thick diameter frame tubes, upright handlebars, at least eighteen gears and wider tires. They are designed for off-road use, although they are often used on paved surfaces. Handling and climbing characteristics vary from model to model.

The hybrid (or cross terrain) bicycle is, as the name suggests, a combination of the road and mountain bicycles. Most models have medium diameter frame tubes, upright handlebars, at least eighteen gears and medium width tires. They are designed to be used on a variety of surfaces. Most new bicyclists are choosing this style for its comfort and versatility.

All three styles are available in tandem versions. Although a quality tandem is fairly expensive, it is an ideal way for two people, especially those of unequal ability, to share a ride. There are a number of shops and rental centers that offer instruction about this special bicycle.

Equipment and Clothing

Bicycle safety begins with the bicycle helmet. There are now dozens of comfortable, economical and effective bicycle helmets. Choose a helmet that matches your fashion style and have it professionally sized and fitted. Wear it every time you get on your bicycle. National research indicates that helmets eliminate over 90 percent of serious bicycling injuries.

While other bicycling clothing often appears strange to the novice, it is very functional and adds to your safety and comfort. Shorts have padding that reduces chafing and numbness. If you feel uncomfortable wearing the skin tight lycra style, there are touring shorts that resemble regular hiking shorts. Gloves are also padded and reduce fatigue and numbness. They also protect the hands from abrasion, in case of a fall. Jerseys have rear pockets and are usually made from lightweight, breathable materials. Shoes have reinforced soles and various pedal attachment systems, in order to increase your comfort and efficiency. If you choose a shoe style with an external cleat, be aware they are not designed for walking more than a few feet. Carry another pair of shoes if you plan on visiting any of the sites included with each tour that require leaving your bicycle. If you plan on bicycling when the weather is colder, there is clothing that provides comfort when the temperature gets well below freezing. In addition, I recommend carrying a lightweight, brightly-colored rain jacket at all times.

Today, bicycle shops are filled from floor to ceiling with accessories. To help you choose from among this baffling array, I have listed those items I consider essential to safety and comfort.

To fix a flat tire and perform minor repairs you need to carry a repair kit, which should include a spare tube, patch kit, tire irons, and a small assortment of tools. To inflate the tire you need a frame mount pump. To provide comfort and prevent dehydration, a water bottle and holder (cage) are essential. A good quality lock is essential if you plan on leaving your bicycle unattended, even for a few seconds. Reflectors and reflective tape should be used at all times, while a good quality lighting system is necessary if you bicycle at night or at dusk. A seat, handlebar, or rack mounted bag (they come in various sizes and styles) is needed to carry the repair kit and other items. You should also carry these essential non-bicycle items: money, personal identification, pertinent medical information and a copy of this book.

You can also choose from a secondary list of accessories. A bell or horn is a good idea, especially if you are riding on a trail used by pedestrians. Fenders eliminate most of the soaking associated with riding in the rain. A rear view mirror gives you more security while riding in traffic. The newest cycling computers not only provide mileage, but have various other features including average speed, current speed, maximum speed, time, pedal cadence and even altitude. An automobile bicycle carrier is a good investment if your trunk is small or you need to carry more than one bicycle.

Maintenance and Riding

Beyond the investment in the proper equipment and clothing, bicycle safety is dependent on equipment maintenance and proper riding behavior. Everyone should learn the rudiments of bicycle mechanics and maintenance. Bicyclists can read a number of good books on the subject or attend a class. These rudiments—which include how to remove a wheel, repair a flat and install a chain—can be learned in a few hours. Before each ride get in the habit of inspecting the bike, paying particular attention to frayed cables, worn or under-inflated tires, metal cracks and broken spokes. Once or twice a year, depending on your mileage, have your bicycle inspected and tuned up by a professional.

Proper riding behavior is essential not only to your safety, but to the continuing endeavor to give bicyclists the respect they are due. Bicyclists have a legal right to use most roads and trails, but with that right comes a responsibility to behave properly. Poor behavior by a few bicyclists can result in increased motorist antagonism and the banning of bicyclists from off-road trails.

If you are new to bicycling, practice on a smooth off-road trail or unoccupied parking lot. Once you have mastered the basics of bicycling, including shifting, braking, riding in a straight line and maintaining a steady cadence, you are ready to bicycle in automobile traffic.

In general, bicyclists are required to follow the same laws as motorists. A complete list of bicycle regulations is available from each state's motor vehicle or bicycle advocate office. Obey all traffic signs and lights. Bicyclists are required to ride with traffic and keep to the right. Learn and use the proper hand signals to indicate turns and stops. Ride single file and maintain a safe distance between you and the bicycle in front. Approach intersections cautiously and establish eye contact with motorists to determine their intentions. When riding off road, yield to pedestrians and signal your intentions and presence.

There are additional guidelines which apply to touring Civil War sites. While riding in parks obey all regulations and the directions of public safety officers. Only ride on paths specifically designated for bicycles. Stay off monuments, cannons and archaeologically sensitive areas. Do not trespass on private property; if uncertain about status, research ownership before proceeding. Be courteous to other visitors and respect the rights of the residents of these areas. Civil War property, whether public or private, is one of America's most important legacies and deserving of everyone's respect.

Although I have made every effort to make these tours as safe as possible, the final responsibility for safety is yours. These tours are often on public roads with automobile traffic and you must exercise proper judgment. The author and publisher can bear no responsibility for any accidents or injury incurred while following these tours.

Maryland

Maryland, in the 1850s, was a microcosm of America. Here, the divergent forces of slavery and the free market came together with industrialization and agriculture. Even though slavery remained strong in the southern counties, the northern and western part of the state never embraced slavery. Baltimore, while politically pro-southern, had strong economic ties with the industrial North. In addition, Baltimore had the fastest growing free black population in the United States.

Marylanders dreaded the approaching conflict and supported compromise, but voted for the pro-slavery presidential candidate, John Breckenridge, in the 1860 election. With Lincoln's victory, compromise was no longer an option, and Marylanders were forced to decide between secession and the Union. After much debate, and military pressure directed by Lincoln, Maryland remained in the Union.

This decision did not spare Maryland from the activities of both Confederate and Union armies. Pro-southern parts of Maryland were occupied by the Union Army and treated almost as harshly as any secessionist state. Confederate forces raided Maryland throughout the war. In September 1862, the Confederate army entered Maryland and the major battles of South Mountain and Antietam were fought. Marylanders served with distinction in both armies. On occasion family members faced each other directly on the battlefield.

Maryland can also be seen as a geographic microcosm of America. Maryland contains a long coastline, the Chesapeake Bay, swampland, parts of two of America's largest rivers, the Piedmont and the Blue Ridge Mountains. The following tours give you the opportunity to explore these varied landscapes as well as Maryland's Civil War history. Maryland has one of America's nicest road and park systems and many strong bicycle advocacy groups. While development has encroached on some historical areas, you will be pleasantly surprised by the unchanged nature of many small towns and the Maryland countryside.

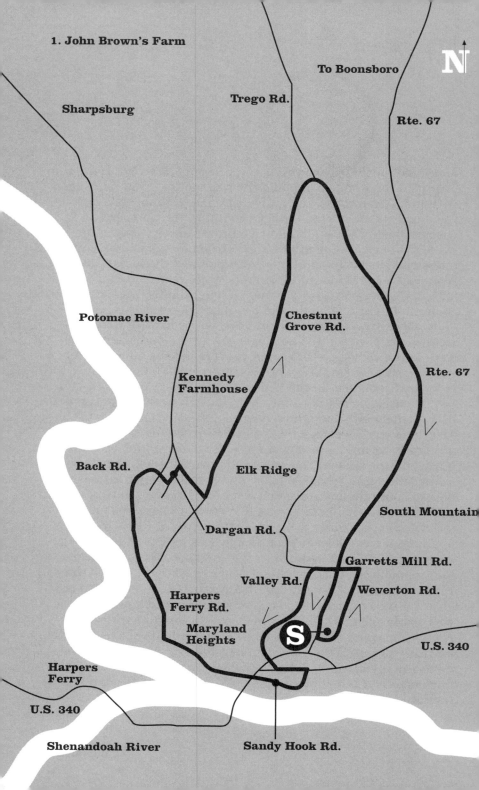

1. John Brown's Farm

To Boonsboro

Trego Rd.

Rte. 67

Sharpsburg

Potomac River

Chestnut Grove Rd.

Rte. 67

Kennedy Farmhouse

Back Rd.

Elk Ridge

Dargan Rd.

South Mountain

Garretts Mill Rd.

Valley Rd.

Weverton Rd.

Harpers Ferry Rd.

Maryland Heights

S

U.S. 340

Harpers Ferry

U.S. 340

Shenandoah River

Sandy Hook Rd.

N

1 John Brown's Farm

Start:
Weverton, Washington County, Maryland; Take Route 340 West to Route 67 North (Boonsboro). Turn right at the first road (Weverton Road). Parking is on the right.

Ride(s):
24.4 Miles, Moderately hilly.

Hike(s):
Weverton Cliffs, 2.5 miles, follow Appalachian Trail blazing and signs from parking lot. Steep ascent and descent. Spectacular view from the cliffs.

Reading:
To Purge This Land With Blood: A Biography of John Brown, Stephen B. Oates, (Harper and Row, New York, 1970)

It is fitting that this is the first ride in this guidebook. On October 16, 1859 John Brown led his tiny army of 18 men from a small farmhouse in Samples Manor, Maryland to Harpers Ferry, Virginia. Brown thought the capture of the town and armory located there would lead to a slave uprising in the area. Eventually Brown thought his army could march to the Blue Ridge Mountains and slaves from throughout the South would join his noble cause. Brown and his followers failed in their martial objective, but his capture and subsequent hanging did succeed in making him the first martyr in the cause of freedom. The Civil War became inevitable after John Brown and his followers invaded Harpers Ferry on that fateful Sunday night.

> *"It was not Carolina, but Virginia, not Ft. Sumter but Harpers Ferry, not Major Anderson, but John Brown who began the war that ended slavery."*
>
> Frederick Douglass

Along this route you can visit the Kennedy Farm, where Brown rented a small house in the summer of 1859 as a base of operations. Here Brown gathered men and arms for the planned rebellion. The house, privately owned and operated, has been restored and is on the National Historic Registry. It is open week-

The Chesapeake and Ohio Canal Towpath. Just south of this spot, John Brown and his men crossed the Potomac and entered Harpers Ferry.

ends and by appointment. Call 301-432-2666 for further information.

This ride also parallels the Chesapeake and Ohio Canal National Historical Park and Potomac River where you can take a short side trip into Harpers Ferry. The ride circles Elk Ridge Mountain (Maryland Heights) and goes through the center of beautiful Pleasant Valley.

There are a few steep climbs during this ride, but the wonderful views are worth the effort. The ride is particularly pleasant in early spring when the Redbud and Flowering Dogwood are in bloom.

Directions:

0.0 Exit parking to right on Weverton Road.

0.1 Left at the yield sign.
You are now heading north, still on Weverton Road. Shift to low gear as you start up the edge of South Mountain. Weverton was founded in 1833 by Caspar Wever as a manufacturing center. The town thrived until the time of the Civil War.

1.3 Left on Garretts Mill Road (unmarked).

1.3 Stop. Cross Route 67 still on Garretts Mill Road.

1.5 Left on Valley Road.
This road was used by Confederate troops moving between Brownsville and Harpers Ferry on September 14, 1862, as part of the Antietam Campaign. Elk Ridge Mountain is on the right. This spur of the Blue Ridge was a critical part of the Union defense of Harpers Ferry. Use caution as you cross a one lane bridge over Israel Creek.

3.6 Stop. Straight across Route 340. Use caution.

3.7 Left on Keep Tryst Road.
A restaurant and store are located at this intersection.

3.9 Right on Sandy Hook Road.
This road starts by going down a steep, winding hill. The road levels off with the Baltimore and Ohio Railroad on your left and the town of Sandy Hook on your right. Many Union troops, including General Grant, used this rail line from Washington to Harpers Ferry during the war. Abraham Lincoln used the train to visit the Union Army in October 1862.

5.0 Cross railroad bridge. Road now is Harpers Ferry Road.
At this point, the Potomac River and C&O Canal National Historical Park are visible on the left. The road narrows as it passes the base of Elk Ridge Mountain on the right. This rocky outcropping is called Maryland Heights and was used by the Union to guard Harpers Ferry. As many as 200 soldiers were needed to haul artillery pieces to the summit. It was captured by the Confederates on September 14, 1862. At 5.9 Miles you can use a wooden footbridge to get to the towpath and cross to Harpers Ferry. Walk your bike across. The road continues up a series of hills around Maryland Heights.

7.8 Left on Back Road.
There is a picnic area and restrooms at 8.6 Miles. At this point the road becomes Shinham Road.

9.7 Continue straight at this stop sign.

9.9 Left on Dargan Road.

10.1 Right on Harpers Ferry Road.
There is a spectacular view from the top of this rise.

10.9 Left on Chestnut Grove Road.
This road was the site of one of the Civil War's most daring escapades. On the night of September 14, 1862, a Union cavalry

regiment under the command of Colonel Benjamin Davis used this road to escape from the Confederates. The Confederates occupied all three heights around Harpers Ferry and the 12,000 man Union garrison was trapped. However, Colonel Davis convinced his commanding officer to allow him to try to sneak by the Confederates in the middle of the night. It was so dark the troopers had to follow the sparks caused by the shoes of the horses walking in front of them. They overran a picket post on this road and the 1,000 man force got past the Confederates without a single casualty. Colonel Davis, who was from Mississippi, fooled a Confederate supply train into following his men into Pennsylvania. Only when the sun rose, did the Confederates discover their predicament.

11.9 Stop. Kennedy farmhouse on the left.
Brown rented this house in July 1859. Posing as a Mr. Smith, Brown quietly gathered his army and supplies here throughout the summer and early fall. Many of the 21 men were forced to hide in the cramped attic during the day, while Brown and his children presented the appearance of a normal family life. Brown acquired more than two hundred rifles and 1,000 pikes for the assault. Allow about 30 minutes for your visit. Exit to left and continue on Chestnut Grove Road. At 13.6 Miles is a small country store.

13.8 Left at intersection. Still on Chestnut Grove Road.

16.1 Right on Trego Road.
On the right is Solomon's Gap. The Confederates used this gap to ascend Elk Ridge on September 12, 1862. Two brigades marched along the spine of the mountain to attack the Union artillery on Maryland Heights from the rear. Starting at about 3:30 p.m. there was a series of skirmishes along the ridge. The terrain was so difficult that soldiers were forced to hold on with one hand, while loading and firing their weapons with the other. The fighting continued on September 13, with the Confederates gaining control of Maryland Heights by the late afternoon.

17.9 Right on Route 67 (Rohresville Road).
You are now heading down the center of Pleasant Valley. This area of small towns and well maintained farms has not changed much since the Civil War. At 18.2 Miles Crampton's Gap is visible on the left. This was the location of heavy fighting on September 14, 1862 (see South Mountain section).

24.1 Left on Weverton Road (unmarked).
This is the last road on the left before the Route 340 overpass.

24.4 Parking on right.

End of tour.

2 South Mountain

Start:
Brownsville, Washington County, Maryland; I-270 or I-70 to Route 340 West. Boonsboro Exit (Route 67 North) to Brownsville. Parking is located at the Brownsville Community Pond, on the right side of Route 67.

Ride(s):
32.6 Miles; Very hilly.

Hike(s):
The Appalachian Trail connects all the sites associated with the Battle of South Mountain. Parking is available at Gathland State Park and Washington Monument State Park. Follow signs and white blaze marks.

Reading:
Before Antietam: The Battle for South Mountain, John Michael Priest, (White Mane Publishing, Shippensburg, PA, 1992)

The Battle of South Mountain (called the Battle of Boonsboro in the South) has been historically obscured for a number of reasons. Historians have studied South Mountain as a part of the Battle of Antietam, which occured three days later and only ten miles west. It seems that this geographic and chronological closeness has kept South Mountain from getting its historical due. In addition, South Mountain's three battlefields, while well-preserved, are separated by a number of miles and ignored by most Civil War tourists.

> *It was a grand and glorious spectacle and it was impossible to look at it without admiration. I had never seen so tremendous an army before, and I did not see one like it afterward.*
>
> Confederate General D.H. Hill, observing the advancing Union army at South Mountain; September 14, 1862

This oversight is unfortunate. South Mountain deserves to be studied as a separate battle with its own implications. The three separate battlefields that comprise South Mountain are as beautiful as any Civil War site, offering stunning views of the

N

Washington Monument State Park

Boonsboro

Zittlestown Rd.

Rte. 34

King Rd.

Washington Monument Rd.

Nicodemus Mill Rd.

Moser Rd.

Turner's Gap

Fox's Gap

U.S. 40

Dogstreet Rd.

Reno Monument Rd.

Rte. 67

Bolivar Rd.

Eakles Mill Rd. (Mt. Brair Rd.)

South Mountain

Marker Rd.

Millbrook Rd.

Mountain Church Rd.

Main St.

Rohresville

Arnoldstown Rd.

Gapland Rd.

Rte. 17

Cramptons Gap

Potomac River

Picnic Woods Rd.

Burkittsville

S

Brownsville

Boteler Rd.

Rte. 67

U.S. 340

South Mountain

To Frederick

Elk Ridge

Maryland countryside. With the continued efforts of historians (the first full length study of the battle has recently been published) and preservationists, perhaps South Mountain will someday get its proper attention.

South Mountain took place on September 14, 1862. After Lee and the Army of Northern Virginia entered Maryland they were pursued by McLellan and the Army of the Potomac. If Lee was to continue north, he knew that he would have to eliminate the strong Union garrison at Harpers Ferry, which threatened his lines into Virginia. In order to remove this threat Lee boldly divided his army into five wings. Three of these wings surrounded Harpers Ferry, while the fourth marched toward Hagerstown and the fifth remained near Boonsboro as a rear guard.

Lee was unaware that a copy of the order delineating these movements had fallen into the hands of Union General McClellan and that the Union army was in pursuit. Lee was forced to block the Union army at the passes over South Mountain with the small force he had at hand. While the Union army was able to force the Confederates off the mountain, the Confederates delayed their progress long enough to capture Harpers Ferry and reunite at Antietam.

This ride is very difficult. In order to tour the sites of some of the heaviest fighting, South Mountain must be ascended at Crampton's, Turner's, and Fox's Gaps. Shift to low gear and take your time. Enjoy the beautiful views and use caution on the steep descents. Completion of this ride is a memorable experience.

Directions:

0.0 Exit parking to right, north on Route 67 (Rohresville Road).
South Mountain is on your right (east) as you ride north through Pleasant Valley. The original Valley road was located to the left of this modern road.

1.4 Right on Gapland Road.
There is a steep climb ahead as you ascend Crampton's Gap. At 2.4 Miles is the top of the climb and the entrance to Gathland State Park. Gathland is named after George Alfred Townsend, one of the Civil War's youngest correspondents. (He used Gath as a pen name). After the war he purchased 100 acres atop the mountain for an estate. In 1896 he erected the War Correspondents Memorial Arch, the only monument in the world dedicated to this important profession.

McLaw's division crossed here and at Brownsville Gap (1.5

The War Correspondents Memorial at Gathland State Park, Maryland.

miles south) on their way to Maryland Heights, overlooking Harpers Ferry. He left just a small force here to guard against the Union advance. At Brownsville Gap he posted a small artillery unit. With the information that a large Union force was advancing from Middletown, additional troops were added including three cavalry regiments under Colonel Thomas Munford.

2.4 Right at Gapland Road (War Correspondents Memorial).

Use caution on steep descent. At 3.1 Miles is intersection with Mountain Church Road. The initial Confederate defensive position was behind the stonewalls to the left, along this road. This was occupied mostly by Munford's dismounted cavalry. The Union, Franklin's VI Corps, attacked on both the right and left of Gapland Road.

The main Union assault started around 3:00 p.m. along a front about a mile wide. The Union outnumbered the Confederates by over 10,000 troops. Soon the Confederates were routed and the fighting proceeded up the slopes of the mountain. Confederate reinforcements, a 1,300 man brigade under

General Howell Cobb arrived from Pleasant Valley, and climbed to the summit. However, they were soon caught up in the rout and driven back into the valley. By 6 p.m. Franklin had won the field, but failed to press his advantage and McLaws was able to put together a defensive line across Pleasant Valley.

3.5 Stop. Left on Potomac Street (Route 17).

Many houses and churches were used as Union hospitals after the Battle of South Mountain. Lincoln reportedly traveled through Burkittsville after visiting Antietam in October 1862. As Union troops advanced through Burkittsville toward Crampton's Gap, they came under Confederate artillery fire. Thomas Hyde of the 7th Maine described the action, " ...cannon balls crashed among the houses, and the women, young and old, with great coolness, waved their handkerchiefs and flags at us."

4.8 Left on Picnic Woods Road.

5.4 Left on Arnoldstown Road.

6.9 Stop. Right on Mountain Church Road.

The Union started their assault on Crampton's Gap in the fields to the left of this intersection. The Confederate 12th Cavalry (dismounted) formed a defensive line across Arnoldstown Road, halfway up the mountain.

7.5 Left at intersection, still on Mountain Church Road.

A cavalry skirmish occured along this road on September 13, 1862. A Federal patrol, pursuing a Confederate wagon train through Middletown Valley, was ambushed by Confederate cavalry who were hidden in the woods to your right.

10.0 Stop. Left on Marker Road.

11.4 Stop. Left on Bolivar Road (unmarked).

12.4 Left on Reno Monument Road.

General McClellan's headquarters was located northeast of this intersection. Artillery and reserves were also located at this spot. The Union assault on Fox's Gap was an attempt to flank the Confederate defense of Turner's Gap, located one mile to the north. At 8 a.m. on September 14th a IX Corps division, about 3,000 men under Brigadier General Joseph Cox, started the steep climb up South Mountain on both sides of this road (called Old Sharpsburg Road at the time of the war).

13.3 Fox's Gap and the Reno Monument.

The battle started at 9 a.m. as the Federals encountered just over 1,000 Confederates, under General Samuel Garland, positioned behind a stone wall north of this spot. The fighting was fierce as the Confederates desperately tried to hold the field and keep the Federals from advancing on Turner's Gap. Garland fell mortally wounded and future U.S. President Rutherford B. Hayes also was wounded leading a Federal charge south of this spot. By 11 a.m. the Union controlled the gap and the surviving Confederates retreated north toward Turner's Gap along a summit road that no longer exists.

The fighting continued north as the Federals pursued the retreating Confederates. Outnumbered and desperate, commanding General D.H. Hill threw together a makeshift line consisting of a few artillery pieces and couriers, teamsters, and cooks along the ridge road. The chicanery worked as the advancing Federals were bombarded with canister. Tired from the mornings fierce fighting, the Federals fell back toward Fox's Gap to await reinforcements.

A resumption in the push toward Turner's Gap started in late afternoon when more troops on both sides arrived. However, the Federals were unsuccessful and as commanding General Jesse Reno neared the summit to scout the action a bullet tore into him. He died in a few minutes. Action here came to a close as the sun fell. Today, only small monuments to Reno and Garland remain as a reminder of the action that took place on September 14, 1862. The Daniel Wise farmhouse was located to your left, as you pass the monuments. Wise was paid a dollar a body to bury Confederate dead. He unceremoniously dumped 60 bodies down his well and sealed it with rocks.

14.0 Right on Moser Road.
This road parallels the summit road that connected Turner's and Fox's Gap during the time of the war. Fighting took place to your right during the afternoon of September 14. This road has many steep climbs.

15.0 Right on Alt. Route 40 (National Pike).

15.2 Left on Washington Monument Road.
This is Turner's Gap. D.H. Hill controlled his difficult defense from this spot. He had to shift troops both north and south as the larger Federal force ascended the mountain from Middletown Valley. As Hill watched the Federals near Mountain House, now the South Mountain Inn, he would later recall, "I do not remember ever to have experienced a feeling of greater loneliness."

In 1876 the Inn and surrounding mountain top became the residence of Madeline Dahlgren, widow of Rear Admiral John Dahlgren. Admiral Dahlgren invented the bottle shaped gun that bore his name and became the standard of Union warships during the Civil War. Their son, Ulric, led an ill-fated cavalry raid on Richmond. On March 1, 1864 Colonel Dahlgren and his raiding party were surrounded and Dahlgren was killed. On Dahlgren's body were papers that the Confederates said detailed a plot to burn Richmond and kill Jefferson Davis and the Confederate Cabinet. The Confederates were outraged and Dahlgren's body was mutilated and buried in an umnmarked grave.

The main Federal assault on Turner's Gap started at 4 p.m. as the I Corps was sent up the mountain. The majority headed north on a flanking march, while one brigade was sent straight up the National Pike. The charge up the National Pike was stalled by a small force of Georgians positioned below the summit behind a stone wall north of the road. Fighting continued in the dark, but the Federals were unable to break the line.

Washington Monument Road leads to Washington Monument State Park. The northernmost fighting of the Battle of South Mountain took place throughout this area. The Confederates were driven back toward Turner's Gap, but at nightfall they still held the National Pike crossing. However, Lee knew he couldn't hold South Mountain when the fighting would resume in the morning and he ordered his troops to withdraw during the night. The Battle of South Mountain was over. The Union sustained 1,800 casualties, while the Confederates lost 2,800 in the three separate fights that comprise the Battle of South Mountain.

16.1 Stop. Entrance to Washington Monument State Park. Left on Zittlestown Road.
The entrance road leads to a short hiking trail, which leads to the Washington Monument. There is a spectacular view from the summit.

17.1 Stop. Right on Alt. Route 40.
Use caution descending steep hill. There are a number of stores and restaurants in Boonsboro. The Boonsboro Museum, which has many Civil War artifacts is located on North Main Street just past the intersection with Potomac Street. It is open Sundays 1–5 p.m.

The battle for South Mountain began and ended with small cavalry skirmishes in downtown Boonsboro. On September 10 a few Confederate cavalrymen, including Stonewall Jackson's aide, Henry Kyde Douglas, were surprised by a Federal patrol. One Confederate, Colonel Bassett French, was forced to hide in a pile of rubbish in the basement of the Boonsboro Hotel. On

September 15, as the Confederate infantry marched toward Antietam, a cavalry regiment remained in Boonsboro as a rear-guard. They soon encountered Federal cavalry and a fierce fight developed along Main Street. The Confederates were forced to retreat on Potomac Street after 20 of their men were killed.

18.9 Traffic light. Left on Potomac Street (Route 34).

19.4 Left on King Road.
On the right is Red Hill. This was used as an observation post and signal station by the Union during Antietam.

20.8 Right on Nicodemus Mill Road.
At 21.7 is a narrow wood-planked bridge. Walk bicycle across.

21.8 Yield. Right on Dogstreet Road.

22.7 Left on Mt. Briar Road (Eakles Mill Road).

25.8 Left on MillBrook Road.
On the left is Mt. Briar Wetlands Park.

26.6 Stop. Right on Main Street (Route 858).
This was an important crossroads during the war. Rohresville has not changed much since October 1862 when Lincoln came through on his way to review the Union troops at Antietam.

27.6 Stop. Right on Route 67 (Rohresville Road).

30.7 Left on Boteler Road. Use caution crossing Route 67.
At 31.6 Miles is St. Lukes Church. Confederate General Lafayette McLaws used it as his headquarters on September 14, 1862. It was also used as a hospital.

31.8 Stop. Right on Route 67.
McLaws established a defensive line across Pleasant Valley at this point, after being driven off Crampton's Gap.

32.6 Parking on right.

End of tour.

3 Antietam

Start:
Sharpsburg, Washington County, Maryland; Route 270 to Route
70 West. Exit 49 -Route 40 Alt.West to Boonsboro. Left on
Potomac Street (Route 34 West). In Boonsboro turn right on
Route 65 and follow signs to Antietam National Battlefield
Visitor Center.

Ride(s):
9.4 and 21.8 Miles; Hilly.

Hike(s):
1.5 Miles; Snavely Ford Trail, this loop trail follows the
Antietam Creek to Snavely Ford, where the Union crossed on
the Confederate right. The trail starts and ends at the Burnside
Bridge and is well-maintained and marked.

Reading:
The Landscape Turned Red, Stephen Sears, (Ticknor and Fields,
New York, 1983)

On September 17, 1862, 87,000 Union troops under General
George McClellan faced 40,000 Confederates under Robert E.
Lee around the town of
Sharpsburg, Maryland. After a
day of fierce fighting, over
20,000 men were killed or
wounded. Antietam would for-
ever be known as America's
bloodiest day.

> *On the first day of January, in
> the year of our Lord one thou-
> sand eight hundred and sixty
> three, all persons held as slaves
> within any state, or designated
> part of a state, the people
> whereof shall then be in rebel-
> lion against the United States,
> shall be then, thenceforth, and
> forever free.*
>
> Abraham Lincoln, The
> Emancipation Proclamation

The debate over who scored
the military victory at Antietam
continues today. Robert E. Lee
considered the entire Antietam
Campaign one of his greatest
achievements. He succeeded in
dividing his army and capturing
Harpers Ferry while being
closely pursued by a much larger foe. Next, he had inflicted
tremendous damages against the Union and was able to with-

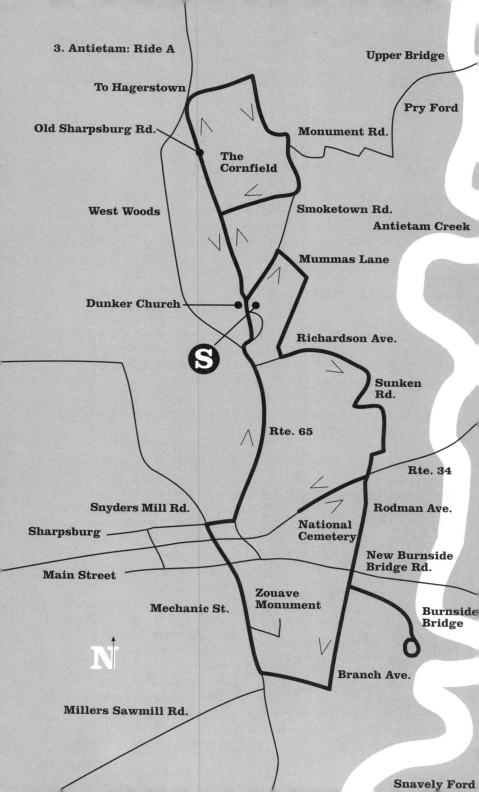

3. Antietam: Ride A

Upper Bridge

To Hagerstown

Pry Ford

Old Sharpsburg Rd.

Monument Rd.

The Cornfield

West Woods

Smoketown Rd.

Antietam Creek

Mummas Lane

Dunker Church

Richardson Ave.

S

Sunken Rd.

Rte. 65

Rte. 34

Snyders Mill Rd.

Rodman Ave.

Sharpsburg

National Cemetery

Main Street

New Burnside Bridge Rd.

Mechanic St.

Zouave Monument

Burnside Bridge

N

Branch Ave.

Millers Sawmill Rd.

Snavely Ford

draw into Virginia according to his own terms.

George McClellan claimed victory because he had prevented Lee from marching into Pennsylvania or turning on Washington or Baltimore. He inflicted devastating losses on Lee's already undermanned army. For once, McClellan crowed, the Union had not been driven from the field.

While military historians have usually called Antietam a draw, the political outcome was a definite Union victory. While the South had Robert E. Lee, the North had Abraham Lincoln, who in one stroke was able to counter much of the South's previous military success. The week after Antietam, Lincoln made public the Emancipation Proclamation, which would become law on January 1, 1863. Despite strong economic pressure, anti-slavery sentiment in England and France would now keep those countries from siding with the Confederacy. In addition, the formation of all black regiments would now be permitted in the Union army. By 1864 these troops would become an important part of the Union army and the defeat of the Confederacy. Finally, while the Emancipation was not the sweeping edict hoped for by abolitionists, it did signal a change in the war's purpose. Now soldiers were not only fighting for the preservation of the Union, but for the end of slavery.

These rides cover the entire Antietam Battlefield, which has been called the best preserved battlefield in America. If you choose the longer ride you will see many of the ancillary sites: including hospitals, troop encampments, and headquarters. If you take your time, and explore all the sites, you will come away with an excellent understanding of one of America's most important and tragic days.

Directions: Ride A

0.0 Exit the Visitor Center parking to your right, north on Old Sharpsburg Road.
Please visit the center before starting your tour. At the center you will receive a map of the battlefield, which you can use to augment this guide. The center has a museum, a painting collection and a bookstore. In addition, there is a short film that is shown every half hour. The center is open every day except Christmas, New Years, and Thanksgiving.

This ride starts by following the National Park auto tour. There are many interpretive markers at important sites, some with audiotape narration. Dunker Church is the first important landmark on your left as you leave the Visitor Center. This was the focal point of the initial Union attack.

The serenity of this winter scene belies the violence that occurred along the Sunken Road (Bloody Lane) on September 17, 1862.

1.0 Right on Mansfield Avenue.

The Union I Corps, under General Joseph Hooker, camped in the fields to the north of this road on the night of September 16. At 5:30 a.m. they swept south into Stonewall Jackson's troops, who were positioned on both sides of the Hagerstown Pike, north of the Dunker Church.

1.7 Yield. Right on Smoketown Road.

The Union XII Corps, under General Joseph Mansfield, supported the I Corps attack by moving south through the fields along Smoketown Road. At the intersection with Monument Road, Mansfield, who had been given command of the XII Corps only two days before, was killed by a Confederate sharpshooter.

1.9 Right on Cornfield Avenue.

The Cornfield, where some of the war's fiercest fighting occured, is to your right.

2.3 Stop. Left on Old Sharpsburg Road.

A Union division, under General John Sedgwick reached the West Woods, which were located on your right. Emerging from the woods (most of the woods don't exist anymore), with their exposed left near the Dunker Church, they were surprised and pushed back by Confederate reinforcements under Jubal Early, Tige Anderson and Lafayette McLaws. Sedgwick lost 2,255 men before he could withdraw across the road.

2.6 Left on Smoketown Road.

2.8 Right on Mumma's Lane (unmarked).
Part of the Federal II Corps veered south from the fighting at the West Woods. At 9:30 a.m. they came through the fields to your left and struck the Confederates.

3.4 Stop. Left on Richardson Avenue.
The Confederate defensive position was centered on the Sunken Road. The parallel fences mark this position to your left as you ride down this road. After four hours of heavy fighting, the Federals finally broke the Confederate line. The heavy casualties on both sides would give the road its historical name—Bloody Lane. Confederate General James Longstreet prevented a total Federal breakthrough by having his staff man artillery on the ridge to your right. An observation tower is located at the end of the Sunken Road.

4.4 Stop. Right on Boonsboro Pike (Route 34). Differs from auto tour.

4.8 Entrance to National Cemetery on the left.
Walk bike across street to entrance. The National Cemetery was dedicated on September 17, 1867. There are 4,776 Union soldiers buried here from the Battles of Antietam, South Mountain and Monocacy.

The Lower Bridge (Burnside Bridge) at Antietam National Battlefield.

4.8 Exit cemetery to right on Boonsboro Pike.

5.2 Right on Rodman Avenue.

5.6 Left on Branch Avenue, which becomes Burnside Bridge Road.

6.2 Burnside Bridge.
The third and final Union assault was launched at this point, starting before noon. A small force of Confederate sharpshooters, posted on these heights, kept Burnside's corps from crossing the bridge until 1 p.m. By 3 p.m. most of IX Corps was across the bridge and ready for the assault towards Sharpsburg. Other Union troops were able to cross at Snavely's Ford, located south of the bridge. (See Hike(s) section.)

6.2 Turn around at parking area and return along Branch Avenue.
The Otto farmhouse is on your left and the Sherrick farmhouse is on your right. Fighting occured in the fields around both these houses as the Federals advanced from the bridge. Both families were forced to flee before the fighting started. Joseph Sherrick hid $3,000 worth of gold in one of his stone walls before fleeing. He recovered it after the battle.

6.7 Stop. Straight on Branch Avenue. (Road did not exist at the time of the battle).
The final Federal attack reached just beyond this ridge. Union General Isaac Rodman was killed by a Confederate sharpshooter while riding through a meadow to your left. He was the ninth Union General to be killed or wounded during the Antietam Campaign. He was trying to warn a Union brigade that Confederates were advancing from the south and west.

These were A.P. Hill's troops who had arrived late in the day after a seventeen-mile march from Harpers Ferry. Except for sporadic skirmishing, Hill's counter-charge brought the Battle of Antietam to an end.

7.6 Stop. Right on Mechanic Street (Harpers Ferry Road). (Turn left for Ride B.)
At 7.9 Miles is a short trail to the 9th New York Zouaves Monument, which marks the apex of the Federal assault on the Confederate right.

8.3 Stop. Straight through intersection with Antietam Street.

8.4 Stop. Straight through intersection with Main Street.

The Civil War's Bloodiest Day takes its name from peaceful Antietam Creek.

Lee held a council of war on the night after the battle in the house on your left at this intersection. A store is on your right.

8.5 Stop. Right on Snyders Mill Road.

8.6 Stop. Left on Sharpsburg Pike (Route 65).

9.4 Right at sign for Visitor Center. Return to parking.

End of tour.

Directions: Ride B

(Follow Ride A directions to Mile 7.6) Left on Harpers Ferry Road.
At 7.7 Miles is Millers Sawmill Road. This road was used by A.P. Hill to march from the Potomac to the battlefield. Lee's chief engineer watched the level of the Potomac from a house at the end of this road.

9.6 Antietam Village.
Use caution crossing one lane bridge over Antietam Creek. The ruins of an iron ore furnace are visible on the right side of the road, east of the bridge. The Union IX Corps camped here after the Battle of Antietam.

10.6 Left on Mills Road.
It is thought that McClellan had his headquarters after

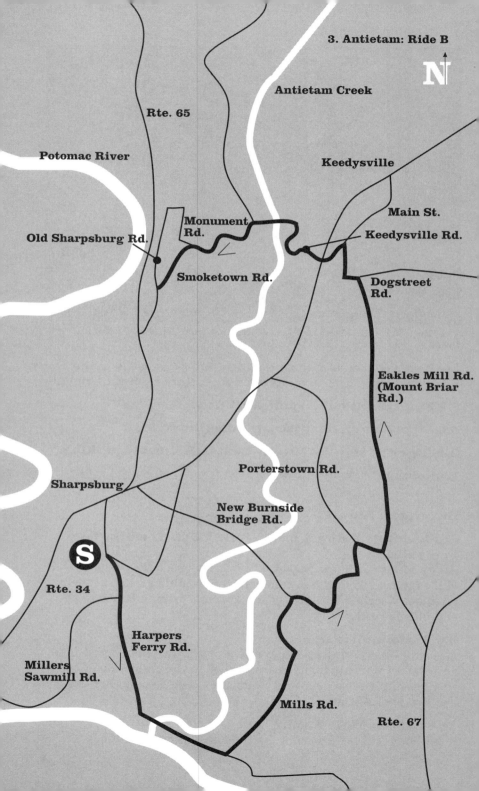

3. Antietam: Ride B

N

Antietam Creek

Rte. 65

Potomac River

Keedysville

Monument Rd.

Main St.

Old Sharpsburg Rd.

Keedysville Rd.

Smoketown Rd.

Dogstreet Rd.

Eakles Mill Rd. (Mount Briar Rd.)

Porterstown Rd.

Sharpsburg

New Burnside Bridge Rd.

S

Rte. 34

Harpers Ferry Rd.

Millers Sawmill Rd.

Mills Rd.

Rte. 67

Antietam at the stone house on your right at 11.6 Miles (unconfirmed). Private Residence.

12.4 Stop. Right on New Burnside Bridge Road.
Two weeks after Antietam, Lincoln visited the area to review the troops, inspect the battlefields and confer with his generals. Lincoln traveled this road from Rohresville and the South Mountain Battlefield to Sharpsburg. Near here, accompanied by General Burnside, Lincoln witnessed a group of hungry soldiers who upset a supply wagon and scrambled for a load of bread strewn across the road. Lincoln watched straight faced as Burnside upbraided the men for their unseemly behavior in front of the commander in chief. This road winds through a hilly area alongside Branch Creek.

14.5 Stop. Right on Porterstown Road.

14.7 Stop. Left on Eakles Mill Road.
At 16.7 Miles on the right is Eakles Mills. Barely visible from the road, this was the home of Martin Eakles. Martin Eakles risked his life bringing ham and biscuits to a Union artillery unit and helping to carry off wounded in his wagon.

17.2 Stop. Left on Dogstreet Road.

17.4 Right on Mount Briar Road.
The house on the right was a small hospital after the battle. A kitchen table was placed in the yard as an operating table. One of the largest Union hospitals was located a half mile to the left on Geeting Road at Locust Spring. The chief Union lookout and signal station was located at the top of Red Hill, one mile to your left. Use caution descending hill to Keedysville.

18.0 Stop. Left on South Main Street.
Many of the buildings in Keedysville were used as hospitals after Antietam.

18.4 Stop. Straight across intersection with Route 34. Use caution. Now on Keedysville Road.
Pry's Mill on the left was a Union hospital, as was the Cost farmhouse on the right. Both are private residences. McClellan's headquarters during the battle was located beyond the ridge on the left at the Pry farmhouse. Access is from Route 34. Use caution as you cross the Hick's or upper bridge. The Union I, XII, VI, and II Corps all crossed the Antietam here and a few hundred yards downstream at Pry's Ford on their way to the battlefield.

18.5 Left on Mansfield Avenue, immediately after crossing bridge.

Use caution as the road narrows and has many sharp turns. This road did not exist at the time of the battle. Union troops advanced across the fields to your left.

21.1 Stop. Left on Smoketown Road.

Entering Antietam National Battlefield.

21.7 Left on Old Sharpsburg Pike.

21.8 Left at Visitor Center parking.

End of tour.

4 Frederick

Start:
Frederick, Frederick County, Maryland; Route 85 North Exit from Route 270 or Route 355 North Exit from Route 70. Route 85 and Route 355 become Market Street in downtown Frederick. Turn right at Church Street. Parking immediately on left, next to Visitor Center. Parking garage has a low clearance, so remove bicycles before parking, if using a bicycle rack on your automobile.

Ride(s):
33.2 Miles; Rolling hills.

Hike(s):
Walking tour of downtown Frederick. A detailed map is available from the Visitor Center. Allow approximately one hour for the two mile tour.

Reading:
Fighting for Time, Glenn H. Worthington, (White Mane Publishing, Shippensburg,PA, 1932-revised 1985)

Frederick, Maryland is probably best known as the location of the the gray-headed Barbara Fritchie's courageous patriotism.

> *Up from the meadows rich with corn,*
> *Clear in the cool September morn,*
> *The clustered spires of Frederick stand*
> *Green-walled by the hills of Maryland.*
> *Round about them orchards sweep,*
> *Apple and peach tree fruited deep,*
> *Fair as a garden of the Lord*
> *To the eyes of the famished rebel horde...*
>
> John Greenleaf Whittier,
> *Barbara Fritchie*

While we now know that Whittier's tale was largely romanticized, his poem remains one of the strongest images of the Civil War. Today, the clustered spires and meadows rich with corn are still visible in and around Frederick. While Frederick has grown tremendously since 1862, it remains one of the best places to still feel the presence of the Civil War.

Frederick's prominence in the Civil War started on April 26, 1861. Less than two weeks after the surrender of Fort Sumter,

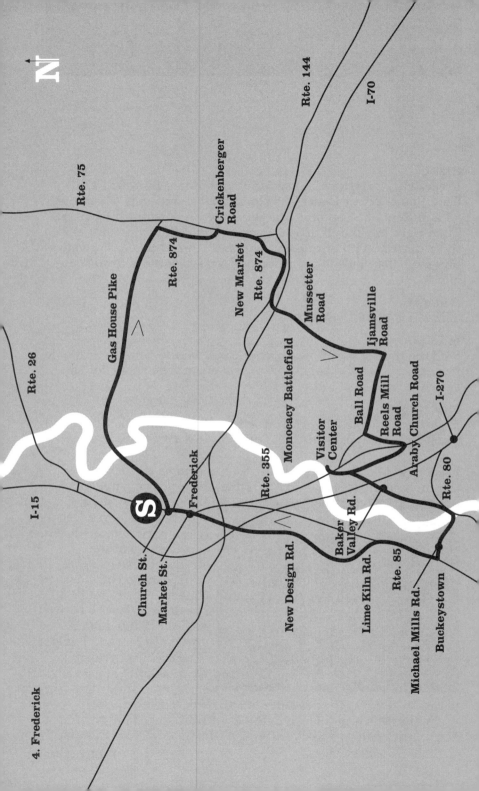

4. Frederick

N

Rte. 75

Rte. 26

I-15

Gas House Pike

Rte. 874

Crickenberger Road

New Market

Rte. 874

Rte. 144

I-70

Mussetter Road

Ijamsville Road

Monocacy Battlefield

Visitor Center

Ball Road

Reels Mill Road

Araby Church Road

I-270

S

Church St.

Market St.

Frederick

Rte. 355

Baker Valley Rd.

New Design Rd.

Lime Kiln Rd.

Rte. 85

Rte. 80

Michael Mills Rd.

Buckeystown

the North was in a state of near hysteria. The Union army was undermanned, underequipped and without proven leadership. Washington, D.C. was isolated and almost completely unprotected. If Maryland decided to secede, Lincoln's government would be completely cut off and the war might be ended before it really started. Sensing this danger, Lincoln called on pro-union Maryland Governor Hicks to call the Maryland legislature into session at Frederick. Here, free from pro-secessionist agitators, the legislature agreed with the governor that Maryland would remain neutral. On September 17, 1861 the legislature met again at Frederick. This time, Lincoln took the extraordinary measure of arresting thirty-one pro-secessionist legislators. They would remain in jail until after the November election, ensuring the election of a strongly pro-union legislature and Maryland's continued Union status.

However, Frederick's Union status would not exempt it from the war's deprivations. The Confederate Army occupied the town in September 1862 on their way to Antietam and in July 1864, during Jubal Early's raid on Washington. Early demanded and received 200,000 dollars from Frederick town leaders in payment for Union destruction of the Shenandoah Valley. The Union Army occupied the town during much of the war, using many buildings for hospitals. Lincoln visited some of the wounded and gave two short speeches in Frederick on October 4, 1862.

This ride starts in downtown Frederick, but in less than a mile you are riding the hills of the scenic Frederick countryside. This rich agricultural area is much the same as it was during the war and it is easy to see why the Confederates came here looking for supplies. The ride continues through New Market and Buckeystown. Both have many antique stores so allow time for browsing or shopping. The ride also goes through the heart of the Monocacy National Battlefield. The Visitor Center has an excellent electric map of the battle.

Directions:

0.0 Exit parking to left. East on Church Street.

0.3 Traffic light. Straight across intersection, road angles to the left and is now called Gas House Pike.

2.1 Gas House Pike crosses Monocacy River.
On July 9, 1862 the Confederates under General Robert Rodes battled Union forces one mile south of this point. The Union defended the Monocacy River Bridge on the National Pike as part of the Battle of Monocacy.

9.2 Stop. Right on London Road (Route 874).

This unique statue in front of the Dr. John Tyler Home on Church Street was stolen by Confederate troops in September 1862 with the intention of being turned into munitions. It was found after the Battle of Antietam and returned and restored.

10.5 Stop. Left on Crickenberger Road.

10.5 Stop. Right on Green Valley Road (Route 75).
This road was patrolled by both Federal and Confederate cavalry in September 1862 and June 1863.

11.4 Right on Old New Market Road (Route 874).

12.2 Stop. Right on Main Street (National Pike-Route 144).
This is downtown New Market. The whole downtown area is on the National Historic Registry. There are dozens of antique stores, a few eating establishments and two bed and breakfasts. New Market grew as a travel stop between Baltimore and Frederick in the 19th century. Today, it is still a hospitable place for visitors. General Fitzhugh Lee's Confederate cavalry patrolled New Market on September 9, 1862. Union General David McMurtrie Gregg's cavalry traveled through New Market on June 28, 1863 on their way to Gettysburg.

13.7 Left on Mussetter Road.

15.8 Enter Ijamsville. Use caution descending steep hill to railroad crossing.

16.1 Left on Ijamsville Road.
Use caution crossing one lane bridge over Bush Creek.

16.8 Right on Ball Road (unmarked).
At 18.0 Miles there is a good view of Sugarloaf Mountain.

19.4 Left on Reels Mill Road (unmarked). This is the second left on Ball Road.

20.4 Stop. Left on Urbana Pike (Route 355). Use caution.

20.5 Right on Araby Church Road.
At the time of the Civil War, this was the main road between Washington and Frederick. There is a view of Frederick and the Catoctin Mountains from this road. As you descend the hill you are entering the Monocacy National Battlefield.

22.3 Stop. Continue straight across Route 355. Use caution.

22.4 Monocacy National Battlefield Visitor Center.
The Battle of Monocacy occured on July 9, 1864. At the end of June 1864, Confederate General Jubal Early launched one of the war's most daring maneuvers. With most of the Army of Virginia hemmed in by Grant at Petersburg, Early would head north with his 15,000 soldiers. Early's goal was to force Grant to divert troops north to cover his march and alleviate some of the pressure on the Confederates at Petersburg. If Grant failed to cover his march, then perhaps Early could invade Washington. On their way the Confederates could seize supplies, food and Federal money.

Grant was slow to believe that Early was going to enter Maryland and turn toward the Capital. Belatedly he sent some reinforcements north, but until that time only General Lew Wallace and a few thousand troops stood between the Confederates and Washington. Starting on July 5 Wallace placed these troops at Monocacy Junction, a logical defensive spot for both Baltimore and Washington. More reinforcements arrived from Grant on July 8. By the time the battle opened on the next morning, the Federals had 5,800 troops positioned along the eastern edge of the Monocacy River. In the ensuing fight the Federals suffered 1,600 casualties and were forced to retreat.

But the Confederates suffered 1,300 casualties and their march on Washington was delayed for a day. By the time they reached the outskirts of Washington, the Federal defenses had been strengthened and Washington was saved. Grant assessed the battle as follows: "General Wallace contributed on this occasion, by the defeat of the troops under him, a greater benefit to the cause than often falls to the lot of a commander of an equal force to render by means of a victory." Allow about a half hour for your visit to the center. A detailed map of the battlefield is available.

22.5 Stop. Recross Route 355. Straight on Araby Church Road.
The Thomas farm is on your right (private property). This important battlefield landmark was used by Federal sharpshooters to slow the Confederate advance from the west.

23.0 Right on Baker Valley Road.
The Pennsylvania and Vermont Monuments are at this intersection. A large portion of the battle took place to your right as you head south on this road. The Federal defensive line stretched from Baker Valley Road to the Monocacy River. The Confederates (Gordon's Division) advanced through these fields after fording the Monocacy.

25.1 Stop. Right on Fingerboard Road (Route 80).

25.9 Right on Michaels Mill Road.(Unmarked, it is the first right after crossing the Monocacy River.)
Use caution as road narrows and bends sharply at Michaels Mill. There is a small park and picnic area between the road and the Monocacy.

27.1 Stop. Right on Buckeystown Pike (Route 85).
The Buckeystown Pike was used by both Union and Confederate troops during the Antietam campaign in 1862. The Union VI Corps camped here on September 13–14, 1862. Robert E. Lee established his headquarters near here on September 7, 1862. There is a store at this intersection.

28.2 Left on Lime Kiln Road.
The farmhouse just north of here on the right was used as a hospital after the Battle of Monocacy. The Confederate flanking march during the Battle of Monocacy was made further north along the Buckeystown Pike. The Confederates marched south on the road and crossed the Monocacy at the Worthington-McKinney Ford. Today, unfortunately, western access to this important historical site is blocked by an industrial park.

29.2 Right on New Design Road. (Unmarked, it's the first right past the railroad tracks.)

30.7 Stop. Straight at intersection with Corporate Drive, still on New Design Road.

31.5 Stop. Straight at intersection with Crestwood Boulevard, still on New Design Road.

32.8 Stop. Left on Market Street. Enter Frederick.
Entrance to Mount Olivet Cemetery is on the left at this intersection. Mount Olivet is the final resting place of Francis Scott Key, Barbara Fritchie, and more than 800 Union and Confederate soldiers. One block further north on Market Street is the Maryland School for the Deaf. On the grounds is the Hessian Barracks which was used as a Civil War hospital. Open by special appointment only. Phone 301-663-8687. At the southeast corner of the next intersection (Market and All Saints Street) was the former location of the train station. From here Lincoln addressed Fredericktonians on October 4, 1862. Lincoln's short speech hinted at his second inaugaral address:

I also return thanks, not only to the soldiers, but to the good men, women, and children in this land of ours, for their devotion in the glorious cause, and I say this with no malice in my heart to those who have done otherwise.

The next intersection (Market Street and Patrick Street) was the site of a skirmish on September 12, 1862. The Confederate rearguard succeeded in driving the pursuing Federal cavalry from the town and took a few prisoners.

33.5 Right on Church Street. Parking on left.

End of tour.

5 Sugarloaf Mountain

Start:
Sugarloaf Mountain, Frederick County, Maryland; Route 270 to Route 109 West (toward Comus). Turn right on Comus Road to base of Sugarloaf Mountain. There are parking areas at the base and at the east and west overlook areas.

Ride(s):
29.7 Miles; Hilly with a few steep climbs.

Hike(s):
Mountain Loop Trail starts at base, follow white blaze marks 2.5 miles. Northern Peaks Trail starts at West Overlook parking, follow blue blaze marks 5 miles. Hikes may be combined. Excellent views, moderate climbing involved.

Reading:
Bold Dragoon: The Life of J.E.B. Stuart, Emory M. Thomas, (Harper and Row, New York, 1986)

Despite increasing development along the I-270 corridor, this remains a "lovely region." Through the efforts of government and private conservation groups, this area of Montgomery and Frederick counties has changed very little since the Civil War. The environmental cornerstone of this region is Sugarloaf Mountain. A conservation-recreation area of over 3,000 acres, Sugarloaf is ideal for hiking, bicycling or just quiet reflection. At 1,282 feet above sea level and 800 feet above the surrounding countryside, this monadnock is the first prominent rise north of Washington, D.C. This geographic fact was not lost on the military during the Civil War. After the Battle of Bull Run (Manassas), both armies settled down to an uneasy peace during the summer of 1861, eyeing each other warily along the Potomac River. They spent the summer training and reorganizing their

> *We are traveling now through one of the most lovely regions I have ever seen, quite broke with lovely valleys in all directions and some fine mountains in the distance.*
>
> General George McClellan in a letter to his wife from his camp near Urbana, Maryland; September 12, 1862

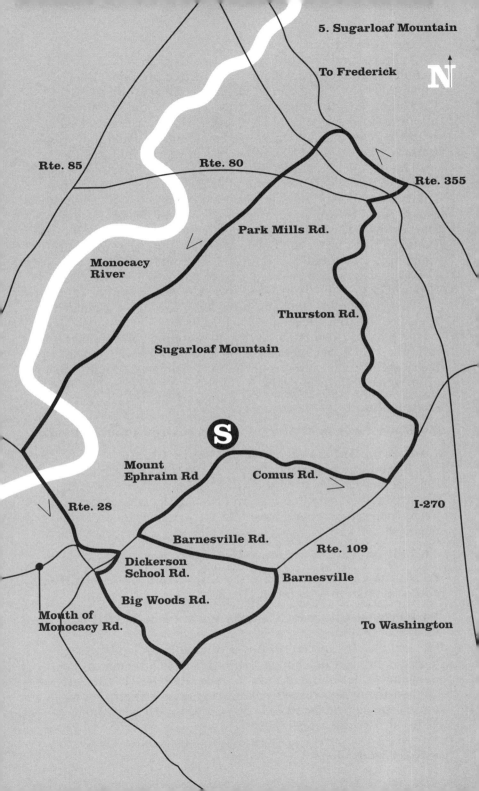

5. Sugarloaf Mountain

To Frederick

N

Rte. 85

Rte. 80

Rte. 355

Park Mills Rd.

Monocacy River

Thurston Rd.

Sugarloaf Mountain

S

Mount Ephraim Rd

Comus Rd.

I-270

Rte. 28

Barnesville Rd.

Dickerson School Rd.

Rte. 109

Barnesville

Big Woods Rd.

Mouth of Monocacy Rd.

To Washington

inexperienced troops.

An important part of Union reorganization was the formation of a Signal Corps. Under the direction of Major Albert J. Myer a system of flag and torch signals was developed. Combined with the telegraph, this system would revolutionize warfare. Rather than rely on dispatch riders, who could take hours to relay a simple message, commanders could now communicate across dozens of miles in a matter of minutes.

The first field training center for the Signal Corps was established on Sugarloaf Mountain on August 31, 1861. From the summit the enemy could be observed in Virginia and their movements could be communicated to stations in Poolesville and Darnestown. It was used throughout the war; soldiers observed Confederates during the Battle of Ball's Bluff, the Antietam Campaign and Jubal Early's July 1864 raid on Washington. The Confederates realized its importance and captured it on September 6, 1862. The Union retook it on September 11.

This ride circles the mountain, going through the small towns of Urbana, Dickerson, Park Mills and Barnesville. These towns have escaped much of the surrounding development and are full of Civil War history. Bring a picnic and enjoy one of the many spectacular views from the top of Sugarloaf Mountain after your exhilarating ride.

Directions:

0.0 Start at base of Sugarloaf. Go east on Comus Road.

2.4 Left on Old Hundred Road (Route 109).
The Comus Inn and a small store are at this intersection. Confederate cavalry used this road on September 5–8, 1862; moving between the Potomac and Frederick. The Union VI Corps followed on September 9, 1862. Excellent view of Sugarloaf.

3.6 Left on Thurston Road. Use caution.

4.7 Right at intersection with Sugarloaf Mountain Road. You are still on Thurston Road.

7.1 Right at intersection with Peters Road. Still on Thurston Road.
The farm at this intersection was originally owned by Roger Johnson, brother of Thomas Johnson (first Governor of Maryland). There was an iron forge located here in the early 1800s. During renovations conducted here a structure was unearthed that might have been part of the Underground Railroad (Private property).

8.6 Stop. Right on Fingerboard Road (Route 80).
Use caution. Watch for turning traffic as you go under Route 270.

9.2 Stop. Left on Urbana Pike (Route 355).
Urbana was the site of one of the Civil War's most amusing stories. Jeb Stuart and his command camped here from September 7–11, 1862. The residents of Urbana, especially the women, were very kind to Stuart and his staff. To repay their hospitality the gallant Confederates decided to organize a ball to be held on the night of September 8, in a girls' academy. The academy was decorated, officers wore their dress uniforms, and guests arrived from the surrounding countryside in fine carriages.

However, the festivities were interrupted by artillery and a messenger saying the Union forces were advancing on one of Stuart's picket posts. Stuart and his men quickly left and, on arriving at the scene of the small skirmish, found that the Union had already been forced to retreat. They returned to the ball at 1 a.m., with tales of the battle and a few wounded. Their wounds were dressed by the women in attendance. The former academy is still standing and can be seen just south of this intersection, across from the Cracked Claw Restaurant.

During his brief stay, Stuart became particularly fond of a woman who was visiting Urbana from the North. Because of her adamant pro-southern views he dubbed her the New York Rebel. When Stuart rode around McClellan's army after Antietam he paid her a brief visit during the night of October 12.

10.7 Left on Park Mills Road.

11.7 Stop. Continue straight on Park Mills Road.
Excellent views of Sugarloaf from this road. Store on right at 13.3 Miles.

14.0 Intersection with Mt. Ephraim Road. Continue straight on Park Mills Road.
Park Mills' history dates from 1785 when Johann Friedrich Amelung started the New Bremen Glass Manufactory just east of here. Although the enterprise failed after a few years, it was an important plant that was the largest of its kind in the newly independent America.

18.3 Stop. Left on Dickerson Road (Route 28).
This road passes the Monocacy Natural Resources Area on your left. A hiking trail here leads to the ruins of an iron forge and lime kiln. At 19.6 Miles on the left (not visible from the road) is Rock Hall. This historic house dates from the early 19th century and was the location of Union troop encampments on September

12, 1862. (Private property). This road was used by both the Union and Confederates on their way to Frederick and eventually Antietam in September 1862.

20.2 Left on Mouth of Monocacy Road.

20.6 Stop. Right on Mount Ephraim Road.

20.8 Left on Dickerson School Road.
Use caution crossing railroad tracks. This railroad line did not exist during the Civil War. Picnic area and restroom located at Dickerson Regional Park.

21.0 Stop. Left on Big Woods Road.
On October 12, 1862 Jeb Stuart's cavalry completed their ride around McClellan's army and crossed the Potomac into Virginia. They were spotted by the signal station on Sugarloaf Mountain and narrowly avoided being trapped by Union cavalry in this vicinity. Only the knowledge of Captain Benjamin White, a resident of the area, allowed Stuart to barely escape the pursuing Federal cavalry.

23.4 Left on Beallsville Road (Route 109).

25.7 Stop. Left on Barnesville Road.
Barnesville changed hands five times on September 9, 1862. Mollie Hays Jones, a fourteen-year-old resident of Barnesville described the Confederate attempt to stall the Federal takeover of the town:

> *These soldiers fixed up a make believe cannon and placed it on the Poolesville Road between the two houses standing at the entrance to the village. This cannon was the two front wheels of a wagon with a big log laid end wise to project over the wheels to look like a cannon.*

Both Confederate and Union forces moved through the town as part of the Antietam Campaign. Confederate Generals Stuart, Fitzhugh Lee, and Wade Hampton were given a meal in one of the town's homes. When the Union followed, Generals Franklin and Abercrombie were shown the same courtesy. After the fighting near town and at the base of Sugarloaf, the wounded were cared for in town. Some of the dead Confederates were buried in the Methodist Cemetery south of town.

27.8 Stop. Right on Mount Ephraim Road.
This is the route the Confederate cavalry took on their way to capturing the signal station on Sugarloaf Mountain. On September 5, 1862 the first official communication of Lee's

crossing the Potomac into Maryland was relayed to Washington from Sugarloaf. The next day, the two officers in charge of the station (Lieutenants Cook and Miner) were captured while trying to return to the station to gain further information. After being paroled by the Confederates the following month, they received commendations for their actions.

On September 10, the 6th U.S. cavalry attempted to take the station back. When half way up the mountain, they were driven off by Confederate infantry and artillery. The next day a larger Union force under supervision of General Winfield Scott Hancock succeeded in retaking the mountain. The wounded from this skirmish were cared for in the small white cottage next to the pond at the base of the summit.

29.7 Parking at base.

End of tour.

Start:
Seneca, Montgomery County, Maryland; Route 270 to Route 28 West. Left on Seneca Road (Texaco station on the left). Left on Riley's Lock Road. Parking at the end of the road, at the C&O Canal Historical Park.

Ride(s):
44.2 Miles; half flat, half rolling hills. A mountain bike or hybrid is recommended because the towpath is not paved.

Hike(s):
The C&O Canal towpath is an ideal hiking trail. There are distance markers every mile.

Reading:
Ball's Bluff, Byron Farwell, (EPM Publications, Inc., McLean, VA, 1990)

While Maryland remained in the Union during the Civil War, its citizens' loyalties were firmly divided. By the end of the war about an equal number of men had served in the armies of the Union and Confederacy. On more than one occasion opposing Maryland regiments faced each other directly in combat.

> *The despot's heel is on thy shore,*
> *Maryland, my Maryland!*
> *His torch is at thy temple door,*
> *Maryland, my Maryland!*
> *Avenge the patriotic gore*
> *That flecked the streets of Baltimore,*
> *And be the battle-queen of yore,*
> *Maryland, my Maryland!*
>
> James Ryder Randall, 1861

Western Montgomery County, known colloquially in the 19th century as the horseshoe of the Potomac because of the wide curve the Potomac takes here, was strongly pro-southern. Many of the citizens of Poolesville and the surrounding area came from Virginia and at the start of the war still had family ties with the Confederacy. While there were few large slaveholders, many farmers had a few slaves and believed strongly in slavery.

The start of the war did nothing to change the allegiance of

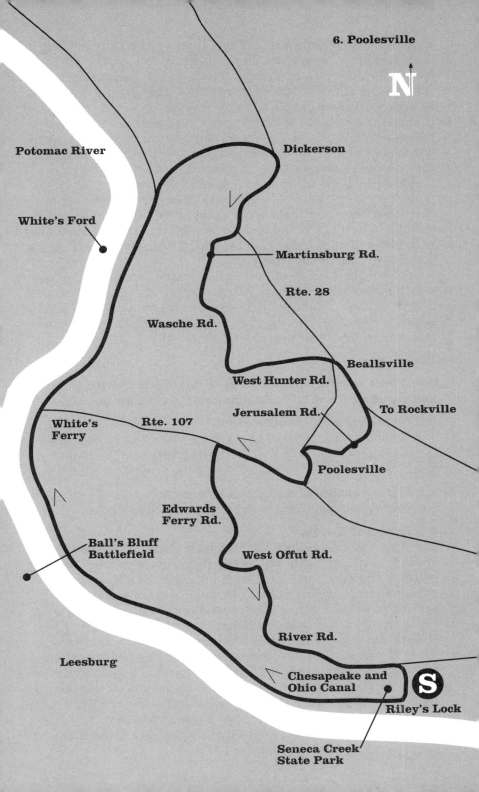

6. Poolesville

N

Potomac River

White's Ford

Dickerson

Martinsburg Rd.

Rte. 28

Wasche Rd.

Beallsville

West Hunter Rd.

Jerusalem Rd.

To Rockville

White's
Ferry

Rte. 107

Poolesville

Ball's Bluff
Battlefield

Edwards
Ferry Rd.

West Offut Rd.

River Rd.

Leesburg

Chesapeake and
Ohio Canal

S

Riley's Lock

Seneca Creek
State Park

these people. By October 1861 there were 15,000 Union troops stationed in the area and Lincoln had imposed martial law. Naturally, this occupation caused tension between residents and Union troops. The troops insulted slaveowners and did nothing to keep slaves from running away. Troops suspected residents of spying and giving aid to the enemy. Crops were confiscated, fences burned and some leading citizens were imprisoned without benefit of a writ of habeus corpus. It is understandable that many people became increasingly hardened toward the Union and would remain bitter for years after the war.

Many young men in the area served in the Confederate army. The most famous of these was Captain Lige White who headed the 35th Virginia Cavalry, known as the Comanchees. He fought with distinction at Ball's Bluff and led a number of raids on his home state, including Poolesville.

The towpath is free of automobile traffic, but please be courteous to hikers and horseback riders. Give warning when you pass and do so slowly. Take your time; there are many historical and natural sites along the way. The ride is nice in summer when the tree canopy and river provide relief from the heat.

Directions:

0.0: Walk or carry bike up small hill to towpath. Start to the right or west (the Potomac will be on your left).

0.5 Seneca Quarry on the right.
This abandoned sandstone quarry supplied stone for the construction of the canal as well as the Smithsonian Castle in Washington, D.C.

3.3 Horsepen Branch campsite on left.
Unreserved campsite and water pump are located here.

8.0 Edwards Ferry.
The Battle of Ball's Bluff, Virginia took place on October 21, 1861. This minor battle had deep political implications. The first battle in the East since the Union failure at Bull Run, it demonstrated the continuing failure of Union military leadership. Started as a demonstration to probe Confederate defenses near Leesburg, it turned into an embarrassing Union defeat.

Lincoln's close friend, Colonel Edward Baker, was killed and many Union soldiers drowned in the Potomac after being driven off a cliff on the Virginia side. On that fateful day two companies of the Ist Minnesota were directed across the Potomac from this spot. They were blocked by the Confederates and were unable to help their comrades at Ball's Bluff further upstream.

70,000 Union troops crossed pontoon bridges here on June 25

and 26, 1863 on their way to Gettysburg. Lige White's command damaged the canal on their way to a skirmish east of here with the 11th N.Y. Cavalry on August 27, 1863.

12.0 Harrison's Island.

Ball's Bluff is located across the Potomac at this point. The main Union force crossed the Potomac here. Their progress was slowed by a lack of boats and the obstruction of Harrison's Island, which splits the Potomac into two channels. This delay contributed to their defeat.

14.7 White's Ferry.

Known during the war as Conrads Ferry, this is the only ferry still in operation on the Potomac. The ferryboat's name, the Jubal Early, reflects the Civil War heritage of the area. The Union maintained Camp Observation here in 1861–62. On December 14, 1862 Lige White and his command captured a number of Union troops in Poolesville and forced them to march to Conrads Ferry before giving them their parole as prisoners of war. There is a store, you can ride the ferryboat for $1.00 roundtrip.

17.2 White's Ford.

This is arguably the most important river crossing of the entire Civil War. From September 4–7, 1862 Robert E. Lee's Army of Northern Virginia crossed here on their first expedition into the North. Ten days later they would battle the Union at Antietam. General Jeb Stuart recrossed the Potomac into Virginia after his second ride around the Union army in October 1862. His rearguard had to hold off the pursuing Union by placing artillery just to the east of the canal. On July 14, 1864 Jubal Early's troops crossed here after their raid on Washington, D.C. There are no markers for this site and it is only visible by following the path south of the power plant to the fishing area next to the Potomac. Follow the bank of the river north until the hills on the Virginia side of the Potomac diminish. This shallow section of the river is White's Ford.

18.7 Spink's Ferry, Lock 27.

This typical canal lock was damaged by the Confederates in September 1862.

19.5 Monocacy Aqueduct

Built between 1829 and 1833, this is the largest aqueduct on the canal. At the time of its construction it was the largest aqueduct in North America. It was built of quartzite, which was quarried at Sugarloaf Mountain and transported to the site by means of a primitive rail system. The National Park Service stabilized the structure after damage caused by Hurricane Agnes in 1972. The Confederates tried unsuccessfully to destroy the structure on September 9, 1862. Confederate General John Walker was given the assignment and later decribed his men's failure, "The attempted work of destruction began, but so admirably was the aqueduct constructed and cemented that it was found to be virtually a solid mass of granite. Not a seam or crevice could be discovered in which to insert the point of a crowbar, and the only resource was in blasting. But the drills furnished to my engineers were to dull and the granite too hard, and ... the attempt had to be abandoned."

If you look closely at the original iron railings you can see grooves worn by years of towropes being rubbed against the ironwork.

19.5 Exit the canal at this parking area.

19.8 Stop. Use caution crossing these railroad tracks.

20.1 Use caution crossing narrow bridge over railroad.
Sugarloaf Mountain, an important Union signal post is visible to the left.

20.9 Right at Dickerson Road (Route 28).

21.3 Store on left.

22.4 Right at Martinsburg Road (flashing light).

22.9 Left at Pepco entrance.

23.6 Left on Wasche Road.

24.9 Left on West Hunter Road.

26.4 Entering Beallsville.
This small crossroads was known as Monocacy Church during the war. The small chapel in the cemetery was vandalized by the Union and used as a stable. Many Confederate soldiers are buried here, including Captain Benjamin White who served as a scout under Jeb Stuart during his ride around McLellan's army in October 1862. His knowledge of the area allowed Stuart to escape the pursuing Union army, part of which was posted on these heights. The cemetery contains a memorial tablet to the Confederate soldiers from the area.

On September 9, 1862 Union cavalry under Colonel John Farnsworth skirmished with the 12th Virginia Cavalry just north of here. They succeeded in driving the Confederates toward Sugarloaf Mountain and captured their battle flag.

26.5 Stop. Right on Darnestown Road (Route 28).

26.6 Straight at intersection of Route 28 and Route 109.

27.6 Right on Jerusalem Road.

28.1 Left at church (still on Jerusalem Road).
This small town probably had its origins in 1861–62. During this time runaway slaves from Virginia were allowed to establish a settlement here, with the tacit permission of Union General Charles P. Stone.

29.3 Stop. Left on Route 109.
The field to your right was the site of a cavalry skirmish on September 8, 1862. On December 14, 1862 the Confederates captured a number of Union prisoners, who were attending Sunday evening service in the Presbyterian Church. This church is on your right as you enter Poolesville. While today Poolesville is a thriving part of Montgomery County, the Civil War took its toll on the town and its inhabitants. A Union regimental history makes the following observation:

> The streets were narrow, and the weather beaten houses were huddled together without order; everything had a tumble-down, decayed appearance. There were two poorly kept taverns, two stores and a church. People came in from the country, mostly on horseback—sometimes the whole family—as many as four riding one horse.

29.9 Stop. Right on Route 107 (Fisher Avenue-White's Ferry Road).
A restaurant is at this intersection and there are a few stores further east on Route 107. A short distance to your left is the John Poole House. Part of the house dates from 1793 when John Poole opened a general store at this crossroads. The town would eventually take his name. Today it houses a Civil War collection and many other 19th-century items. It is open weekends year-round. A state historical marker, describing the area's significance during the Civil War, is on your left as you head out of Poolesville.

Colonel (also Senator) Edward D. Baker's body was brought to the building at the intersection of Route 107 and Willard Road for burial preparation after he was killed at Ball's Bluff. News of Baker's death was telegraphed from Poolesville directly to Lincoln in Washington. Tears came to Lincoln's eyes upon hearing of Baker's death. One of Lincoln's oldest friends, he had named one of his sons for Baker. Lincoln would suffer many more personal losses before the war was over.

32.0 Left on Edwards Ferry Road.
Camp Heintzelman, a major Union encampment, was located at this intersection during the winter of 1862–63.

33.9 Right at intersection (still on Edwards Ferry Road).
Another Union camp was located on the fields to your right as you ride down Edwards Ferry toward the river. Oliver Wendell Holmes, Jr. was stationed here in 1861.

35.2 Left on West Offut Road.

35.9 Road bends to right and becomes Mount Nebo Road.
Mount Nebo contained artillery emplacements in 1861. Use caution on the steep descent as the road twists and narrows.

37.4 At the bottom of the hill, the road becomes River Road.
McKee Beshers Wildlife Manangement Area and Seneca Creek State Park are to your right.

42.8 Seneca Schoolhouse Museum is on your right.
Built in 1866 the schoolhouse is a good example of the educational conditions that prevailed after the war. It is open Sunday afternoons from March 15 through December 15.

43.5 Right on Riley's Lock Road.

44.2 Return to parking area.
This shallow section of the Potomac is Rowser's Ford. Jeb Stuart's cavalry crossed here on June 28, 1863. He captured a wagon train at Rockville and then headed north toward a meeting with the main Confederate army on July 2 at Gettysburg.

End of tour.

Start:
Westminster, Carroll County, Maryland; Route 70 to Route 27
North (Mount Airy Exit). Make right after second traffic light
(Main Street) in downtown Westminster to Locust Street
Parking Lot.

Ride(s):
25.5 and 40.9 Miles; Hilly.

Hike(s):
Two walking tours of downtown Westminster. Detailed maps are
available at the Westminster Visitor Center at 210 East Main
Street. Walking both tours takes about two hours.

Reading:
*Just South of Gettysburg: Carroll County, Maryland in the Civil
War*, Frederic Shriver Klein–Editor, (The Newman Press,
Westminster, MD, 1963)

History is both the study of what occurred and the debate over
what might have happened. A trip to Carroll County, Maryland
gives you the opportunity to
ponder two such cases of possibility. After completing one or
more of these tours you will
realize how fragile history is
and how a few minutes or a few
miles can change its entire
course.

*If the enemy assume the offen-
sive, and attack, it is [General
Meade's] intention, after
holding them in check
sufficiently long, to withdraw
the trains and other
impediments; to withdraw the
army from its present position,
and form line of battle with the
left resting in the neighborhood
of Middleburg, and the right at
Manchester, the general direction being that of Pipe Creek.*

General Meade's Pipe Creek
Order; July 1, 1863

The last days of June 1863
found the Confederate infantry
probing into southern
Pennsylvania without the benefit of Jeb Stuart's cavalry. Lee
had given Stuart permission to
cross into Maryland, but had
specifically ordered Stuart to
rejoin the infantry as soon as
possible. However, Stuart

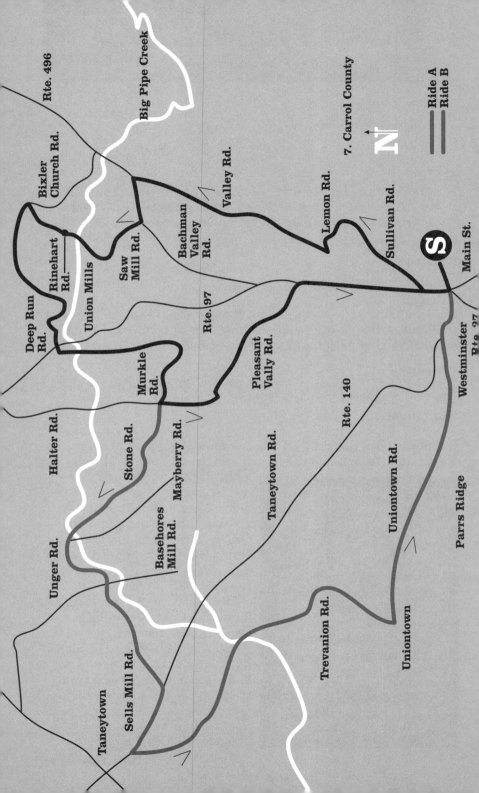

Rte. 496

Bixler Church Rd.

Big Pipe Creek

7. Carrol County

Ride A
Ride B

N

Valley Rd.

Lemon Rd.

Deep Run Rd.

Rinehart Rd.

Union Mills

Saw Mill Rd.

Bachman Vally Rd.

Sullivan Rd.

S

Rte. 97

Murkle Rd.

Pleasant Vally Rd.

Main St.

Westminster

Rte. 27

Halter Rd.

Stone Rd.

Mayberry Rd.

Taneytown Rd.

Rte. 140

Uniontown Rd.

Unger Rd.

Basehores Mill Rd.

Parrs Ridge

Taneytown

Sells Mill Rd.

Trevanion Rd.

Uniontown

became caught between the pursuing Union forces and was further delayed by the capture of a Union wagon train at Rockville, Maryland on June 28. By the afternoon of June 29 the vanguard of Stuart's force reached Westminster. At the intersection of Main Street and Washington Road they encountered a small force of Union cavalry (1st Delaware Cavalry). While the Union forces were quickly routed, Stuart was further delayed rounding up prisoners and taking care of casualties. Stuart spent part of the night sleeping on a chair in front of a store in downtown Westminster. However, a much larger Union force was in pursuit of Stuart and his rest would be brief. His force left Union Mills after breakfast on June 30. The Union would arrive here just hours after his departure. After a major cavalry skirmish at Hanover, Pennsylvania Stuart was forced further east and north in search of the rest of Lee's army. He wouldn't arrive at Gettysburg until the fight was well under way on July 2. This separation has been the cause of continuous debate. What if Stuart would have arrived earlier? Would his presence have altered the outcome of the Battle of Gettysburg? You decide.

> . . . judge whether you can pass around their army without hindrance, doing all the damage you can, and cross the river east of the mountains.
>
> General Lee's order to General Stuart; June 23, 1863

The second debate concerns the location of America's most famous battle. General George Meade, who had only been in charge of the Army of the Potomac for one week, was unsure of Lee's motives. However, Meade knew he had to keep his army between Lee and Baltimore and Washington. He had his engineers select a strong defensive position that would enable the Union to maintain its supply lines via Westminster. They selected a line running southwest to northeast, paralleling Parr's Ridge and Pipe Creek. There is a good chance Gettysburg might have been fought along this line if the two armies had not met by chance on July 1, west of Gettysburg. If this had occurred, students would have to remember facts concerning the Battle of Westminster or Pipe Creek.

Both rides start in downtown Westminster and follow back roads to historic Union Mills. After taking a break here proceed west along some more scenic back roads. At this point, you can decide to continue further west to Taneytown and Uniontown or south to Westminster. Either ride is full of scenery, history and enough hills for a full day's workout.

Directions: Ride A

0.0 Turn right on Main Street at intersection of Main Street and Railroad Street.

0.3 Right at Pennsylvania Avenue (Route 97).
Western Maryland College is to the left. On June 28, 1863 the 1st Delaware Cavalry made their headquarters on this hill.

1.0 Right on Sullivan Avenue.

1.2 Stop. Left, still on Sullivan Avenue.

1.2 Stop at light. Continue straight across Route 140, still on Sullivan Avenue.
This area of orchards and dairy farms has remained largely unchanged since the Civil War. A Union soldier, on his way to Gettysburg, commented on this landscape:

> *The rich farms, the fields of clover and of waving grain, nearly ripe for the harvest, the commodious barns, the comfortable dwellings, and the general prosperity; all stood out in contrast to the region (Virginia) we had just left.*

3.1 Left on Lemmon Road.

3.8 Stop. Right on Old Bachman Valley Road.

5.3 Left at intersection with Fridinger Road, still on Old Bachman Valley Road.

7.5 Stop. Left on New Bachman Valley Road.
Use caution. Moderate high speed traffic on this road.

8.3 Right on Saw Mill Road East.
This road enters the Hashawa Environmental Center.

9.6 Road bends sharply to the right, becomes Rinehart Road. At 10.2 the road crosses Big Pipe Creek, the heart of Meade's proposed defensive line.

11.6 Left on Bixler Church Road.
Use caution. Steep descent to stop.

11.8 Stop. Left on Deep Run Road East.

14.6 Stop. Left on Old Hanover Road.
This road was used by Jeb Stuart's cavalry on June 30, 1863 on their way from Union Mills to Hanover. T. Herbert Shriver, who lived at Union Mills, helped lead Stuart on his way. Because he was only sixteen, Stuart had to ask Shriver's mother's permission and promised him a commission at the Virginia Military Institute

in payment for his service. T. Herbert Shriver did attend the Institute and participated in the Battle of New Market in 1864.

14.8 Stop. Right on Littlestown Pike (Route 97).
Before proceeding on Littlestown Pike, visit Union Mills Homestead and Gristmill. The homestead is located across Big Pipe Creek to your left. Please walk your bike across the narrow bridge. Union Mills is open May through October on weekends; 12–4 p.m. Call 410-848-2288 for more information.

The Shriver family (who still own and operate the mill and homestead) were divided by the Civil War. Andrew Shriver owned the homestead and a tannery. Although he owned slaves, he supported the Union and two of his sons served in the Union army. Henry fought the Confederates on June 26, 1863 at Gettysburg. Andrew Shriver's brother William owned a neighboring property and ran the gristmill. Four of his sons fought for the Confederacy, including the aforementioned T. Herbert Shriver. The war reached the homestead on the evening of June 29, 1863 with the arrival of Jeb Stuart's cavalry. These troops arrived all night and kept the Shrivers busy cooking and entertaining. The Union V Corps arrived early that same afternoon. They camped around the still smoldering Confederate campfires.

15.3 Left on Murkle Road.
Store on left at this intersection. At 15.6 Miles road crosses Big Pipe Creek.

17.4 Stop. Right on Stone Road.

18.8 Left on Halter Road. (Continue straight for Ride B.)

19.5 Left on Pleasant Valley Road.
It is conceivable that Meade would have established his headquarters near this small town, if the battle occurred along Pipe Creek.

19.8 Straight through intersection with Hughes Road.

22.7 Stop. Right on Littlestown Pike (Route 97).
Use caution. Moderate high speed traffic, stay to right on shoulder and watch for merging traffic.

24.3 Straight through Route 140 intersection. Use caution.

25.2 Stop. Left on Main Street.

25.5 Left on Railroad Street. Return to parking area.

End of tour.

Directions: Ride B

Follow instructions for Ride A to Mile 18.8; continue straight on Stone Road.

22.6 Left at intersection with Flickinger Road, still on Stone Road.

23.7 Stop. Left on Mayberry Road.

23.9 Right on Unger Road (just over Pipe Creek).
This scenic road follows Pipe Creek. Use caution as the road narrows past the dairy farm.

25.2 Stop. Right on Basehores Road.

25.2 Left on Sells Mill Road.

27.5 Stop. Right on Baltimore Street (Route 140).
Enter downtown Taneytown. Taneytown was the headquarters of Union General Meade on June 29–July 1, 1863. From here he received news of the start of the Battle of Gettysburg and decided to order the Union army north to meet the Confederates. Both the II and III Corps camped here on their way to Gettysburg. There are a number of stores and restaurants in Taneytown.

28.5 Left on Trevanion Road. Use caution. Yield to oncoming traffic.
The Antrim Inn is on the left as you make the turn.

34.0 Stop. Left on Uniontown Road.
Uniontown's main street is a preservationist's dream. About twenty buildings have been restored to their original 19th century appearance. A guide detailing each structure's history and architec tural significance is available from the Westminster Visitor Center.
Confederate Colonel Rosser and his Cavalry Regiment passed through this town during the Antietam Campaign. The Union II Corps camped one mile east of town on June 29, 1863. Their commander, General Winfield Scott Hancock, stayed at the home of Dr. J.J. Weaver at 3406 Uniontown Road. Many members of his staff stayed at the old Uniontown Hotel at 3477 Uniontown Road.

40.0 Stop. Continue straight across New Windsor Road.

40.4 Stop. Continue straight across Doyle Road.

40.4 Yield. Merge with Main Street.

40.9 Stop. Left on Railroad Avenue. Return to parking area.

End of tour.

8 Fort Washington–Fort Foote

Start:
Fort Washington National Park, Prince George's County, Maryland; I-95 to Exit 3B, Indian Head Highway (Route 210) South. Right on Fort Washington Road. Road ends at entrance to Fort Washington National Park. Admission is charged.

Ride(s):
17.9 Miles; Flat, with a few small hills.

Hike(s):
2 Miles; no formal trail, but a series of paths circle the park. A map is available from the Visitor Center.

Reading:
Mr. Lincoln's City: An Illustrated Guide to the Civil War Sites of Washington, Richard M. Lee, (EPM Publications, Inc., McLean, Virginia, 1981)

After the Union defeat at Bull Run, Lincoln called for George McClellan to take control of all Federal troops in and about Washington. While McClellan was prone to exaggeration, the situation he encountered on his arrival was indeed desperate. Many troops roamed the streets of Washington drunk and without valid passes. A few regiments threatened mutiny. Roads and waterways leading to Washington were guarded by only a few undermanned posts.

> *I found no army to command. There was a mere collection of regiments cowering on the banks of the Potomac, some perfectly raw, others dispirited by the recent defeat. The city was almost in condition to have been taken by a dash of a regiment of cavalry.*
>
> General George McClellan, writing later about conditions in Washington, D.C. on July 26, 1861

Lincoln had appointed the right man for the formidable task of stabilizing the Union army and securing the safety of Washington. McClellan was an organizational genius and a master of delegation. In a matter of weeks he arrested troublemakers, re-established discipline and returned morale to the beleaguered troops.

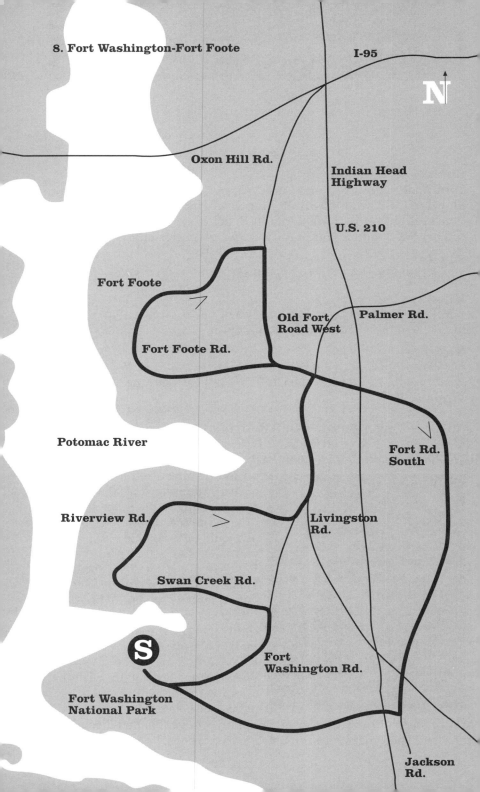

8. Fort Washington-Fort Foote

I-95

N

Oxon Hill Rd.

Indian Head
Highway

U.S. 210

Fort Foote

Old Fort
Road West

Palmer Rd.

Fort Foote Rd.

Potomac River

Fort Rd.
South

Riverview Rd.

Livingston
Rd.

Swan Creek Rd.

S

Fort
Washington Rd.

Fort Washington
National Park

Jackson
Rd.

For the task of securing Washington's defense, McClellan appointed Major John G. Barnard. Barnard, a 47-year-old engineer, enlisted over 3,000 soldiers and civilians in the task of constructing a ring of forts, roads and entrenchments around Washington. Within a few months, dozens of forts were constructed and fitted with artillery pieces. By 1865, 68 forts were constructed and occupied by over 30,000 troops. Washington became the most heavily fortified city in the world.

This ride connects the two most southern forts in Maryland. Fort Washington has its origins from before the War of 1812, while Fort Foote was constructed from 1863–1865. Both forts are well-preserved and have commanding views of the Potomac and Washington. While much of the ride goes through a heavily developed section of Prince George's County, there are other areas that are still farms and woods. Roads are generally wide, with low speed limits and signs telling motorists to share the road with cyclists.

Directions:

0.0 Start at Fort Washington Park. Exit on Fort Washington Road. Start odometer at exit.
On weekends there are living history demonstrations pertaining to the Civil War at the park. Call 301-763-4600 for a schedule of events so you can plan your ride to coincide with one of these interesting events. Before starting your ride go to the park Visitor Center (the two-story yellow building next to the parking area). The center has literature and maps pertaining to both forts, and a small museum and bookstore.

1.7 Left on Swan Creek Road.
At 2.6 Miles you cross over Swan Creek; there is a marina on your left.

3.0 Stop. Right on Riverview Road.
There are still some farms and orchards remaining along this road. There are views to the left of the Potomac River and Broad Creek. The many narrow and winding creeks leading to the Potmac were used by the pro-southern residents of the area for smuggling. Here they could hide their small, shallow draft boats from the Union troops stationed in the area. At night they would slip across the Potomac, carrying mail, newspapers and information concerning Union troop movements.

4.0 Road bends sharply to the right.

5.0 Traffic Light. Left on Fort Washington Road.
Use caution going down hill to town of Silesia.

5.7 Traffic Light. Left on Livingston Road.

6.6 Stop. Left on Fort Road West.
Shopping center at this intersection.

7.1 Traffic Light. Left on Fort Foote Road.

8.7 Left at entrance to Fort Foote Park. Short dirt road leads to park.
The fort was named for Rear Admiral Andrew Hull Foote, who died in 1863 from wounds received while attacking Fort Donelson on February 14, 1862. The remains of the fort's earthen walls are still visible and there are two fifteen-inch Rodman cannons still in place. Under the direction of Colonel Henry Seward, the 9th New York Artillery could use these enormous guns to launch a 440 pound shell three miles downstream. Fort Foote was the last active fort in the Washington area built for the Civil War. It was finally deactivated in 1878.

Interpretive signs explain the fort's activities and the location of various buildings. There is a picnic area and a short trail leading down the hill to the Potomac River.

8.7 Exit park to left, continue on Fort Foote Road.

10.1 Stop. Right on Oxon Hill Road.

11.7 Stop. Straight on Old Fort Road West.

11.9 Stop. Straight across Indian Head Highway, continue on Old Fort Road West. Becomes Fort Road South.

15.3 Stop. Straight across Livingston Road, continue on Old Fort Road South.
Store at this intersection.

15.7 Stop. Right on Old Fort Road South (Jackson Road intersection).

15.9 Traffic light. Straight across Indian Head Highway, still on Old Fort Road South.
This section of Old Fort Road winds through a hilly wooded area. Use caution as the road narrows.

17.5 Stop. Left on Fort Washington Road.

17.9 Fort Washington Park entrance.

End of tour.

9 John Wilkes Booth's Ride

Start:
Cedarville State Forest, Charles County, Maryland; I-95 to Exit 7–Route 5 South. Route 5 joins Route 301 South. Left on Cedarville Road (sign for Cedarville State Forest). Right on Bee Oak Road to Visitor Center parking on the right.

Ride(s):
19.4 Miles; Flat.

Hike(s):
Over fifteen miles of marked trails located in Cedarville State Forest. The swamp trail is of particular interest to this ride as it passes through the Zekiah Swamp (2 miles). This trail is often wet so wear proper footwear.

Reading:
John Wilkes Booth Himself, Richard Gutman and Kellie Gutman, (Hired Hand Press, Dover, Massachussetts,1979)

Abraham Lincoln had to face the possibility of assassination from the beginning of his presidency. On his way to Washington after his election, detectives uncovered an assassination plot by Southern sympathizers in Baltimore. Lincoln changed his itinerary and removed his top hat to make himself less noticeable while changing trains in Baltimore. Sharpshooters were posted in the windows of the Capitol during his inauguration on March 4, 1861. In the summer of 1862 an assassin's bullet passed through Lincoln's top hat while he was riding from the White House to the Soldiers Home, in north Washington.

> *When I leave the stage, I will be the most famous man in America.*
>
> John Wilkes Booth to a drinking companion, shortly before entering Ford's Theater on April 14, 1865.

Threats increased as the Confederate cause became more desperate. By 1865 Lincoln had collected over 80 letters containing death threats. Huge sums of money were offered publicly in the South for his assassination.

However, except for a few common sense precautions Lincoln

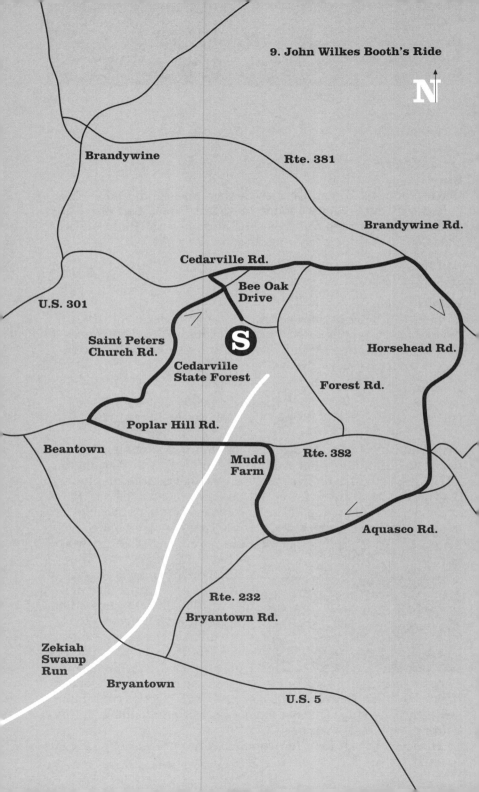

9. John Wilkes Booth's Ride

did not let the threats alter his routine. He reasoned, "If anyone is willing to give his life for mine, there is nothing that can prevent it." He continued to walk around Washington with only a few bodyguards, and occasionally he even slipped away from them to walk to the War Department alone.

The course of events that brought John Wilkes Booth and Abraham Lincoln together may have started as early as 1859, when Booth visited Charles Town, WV in order to be present at the execution of John Brown. While Booth despised Brown's attitude toward slavery, he may have been impressed with Brown's determination to martyr himself for a cause. During the war Booth didn't serve in the Confederate army, but he did help smuggle supplies to the South.

By 1864 Booth started to formulate plans for the kidnapping of Lincoln in order to obtain the release of thousands of Confederate prisoners of war. For a number of reasons, this plan evolved into assassination by the spring of 1865. Booth and his conspirators planned to assassinate Lincoln, Vice President Andrew Johnson, and Secretary of State William Seward. Only Lincoln would die from their efforts on that night.

Booth and one of the other conspirators, David Herold, fled south after the assassination. This ride follows their flight through the Maryland countryside. Here they got medical assistance for Booth's broken leg and hid from their pursuers with the help of Southern sympathizers in the area before crossing the Potomac to Virginia. This area of small towns, forests, and swampland is ideal for bicycling and hiking. Enjoy the quiet roads as you pedal and hike through an area that contains an important part of our Civil War history.

For additional information visit the Mary Surratt House at 9110 Brandywine Road, Clinton, Maryland (301-868-1121). They conduct annual bus tours retracing Booth's escape route.

Directions:

0.0 Exit parking area to left, north on Bee Oak Road.
Cedarville State Forest contains 3,510 acres. The headwaters of the Zekiah Swamp, Maryland's largest, are located in the park. Because much of the surrounding land is wetlands it remained untouched by agriculture and development. Moonshiners, smugglers, and southern sympathizers were able to hide in the swamp during the Civil War. Booth and Herold ventured into the swamp on April 15, 1865.

1.0 Stop. Right on Cedarville Road.
At 2.8 Miles there is a store on the left.

3.7 Stop. Right on Brandywine Road (Route 381 South).
Booth and Herold used this road, traveling between T.B.(a small
village just west of Brandywine) and Dr. Mudd's house, north of
Bryantown. By the time they reached this point, it was probably
after 2 a.m. on the morning of April 15, 1865.

5.2 Right on Horsehead Road.
The small village of Horse Head was located at this intersection.
You are still following the route of Booth and Herold. As they
passed through Horse Head, Booth must have been in horrible
pain. He had been on horseback for over four hours with only
one brief stop and a glass of whiskey to ease the pain of his broken fibula.

**7.8 Stop. Straight through intersection with Poplar Hill
Road, still on Horsehead Road.**
Booth and Herold turned right at this road.

8.5 Stop. Right on Aquasco Road.

**9.7 Use caution crossing railroad tracks, continue
straight at Gallant Green Road intersection.**

**11.1 Straight at Bryantown Road intersection, Aquasco
Road becomes Bryantown Road at this point.**
Bryantown is located 3 miles south of this point. Booth first met
Dr. Mudd while attending a Catholic church service in
Bryantown in November 1864. Booth stayed at Mudd's house
that night and the next day purchased a horse from one of
Mudd's neighbors. The horse was stabled in Washington and
ridden by Booth after the assassination.

12.6 Left at entrance to Dr. Samuel A. Mudd Farmhouse.
The Mudd House is open from noon to 4 p.m. on Saturday and
Sunday from April through November. There is an admission
charge. Allow about one hour for your visit. The house has been
returned to its 1865 appearance and contains many original
pieces of furniture, including the couch Booth sat on while
Mudd splinted his broken leg. Costumed docents give an account
of that night and Mudd's subsequent arrest and imprisonment.
While Dr. Mudd and his descendants would maintain his inno-
cence in the conspiracy, there are certain facts that have gone
undisputed. Booth and Herold arrived at Dr. Mudd's farm at 4
a.m. on April 15. Mudd sliced off Booth's riding boot, which was
found by the authorities later, and put a makeshift wooden
splint on the leg.

In the early afternoon, Herold and Mudd went to Bryantown
in search of a carriage, which would cause less pain to Booth on
his journey south. For reasons still unknown, Herold didn't con-

tinue to Bryantown and told Mudd that Booth and he would continue on horseback. Mudd continued to Bryantown, where he went to the post office and where, he testified later, he received news of Lincoln's assassination. By 4:00 p.m. Booth and Herold had left the Mudd farmhouse, riding off into the gloom of the Zekiah Swamp.

A visit to the farmhouse gives you the opportunity to learn about Mudd's subsequent arrest and imprisonment and the interesting story of his pardon for treating yellow fever victims at the prison. The debate over Mudd's role in the conspiracy continues and after you leave the farmhouse you can ponder the evidence as you finish the ride.

13.0 Stop. Left on Poplar Hill Road.

15.2 Right on Saint Peters Church Road.
If you continue straight at this intersection, you will enter the small village of Beantown. When Booth fled Ford's Theatre he was confronted by Sergeant Silas T. Cobb, who was guarding the Navy Yard Bridge, which was located at the foot of 11th Street in Washington. The bridge was supposed to be closed after 9 p.m., but now that the war was coming to a close the regulation was not strictly enforced. Cobb confronted Booth and asked his name and destination. Surprisingly, he answered "Booth" and said his destination was his home near Beantown.

18.5 Stop. Right on Bee Oak Drive.

19.4 Parking on right.

End of tour.

West Virginia

The Civil War created West Virginia. When a Virginia convention met in Richmond in April 1861 and voted for secession, the delegates from the western part of the state, whose economic interests differed greatly from slaveholders, opposed the ordinance by ten to one. These delegates met in Wheeling and had their own convention in November 1861. This convention drafted a constitution, which was ratified by popular vote in 1862. West Virginia formally entered the Union on June 20, 1863.

However, all residents of this new state were not pro-Union. 30,000 West Virginians served in the Union army, while 10,000 served in the Confederate army. In particular, the area of the Eastern Panhandle was strongly pro-southern. In 1871, Jefferson and Berkeley counties petitioned the United States Supreme Court for the right to return to Virginia. Their motion was denied.

Included in this chapter are two rides in the Eastern Panhandle. They take place in and around two of West Virginia's oldest and most historic cities, Harpers Ferry and Shepherdstown. I have not included western West Virginia because this area was outside the geographic scope of this book. However, I encourage you to do your own exploration of this area. Almost 600 military engagements took place in West Virginia during the war. While many were minor skirmishes, others are important and worthy of further study.

Today, West Virginia has become a leader in Civil War and bicycling tourism. They have developed the most extensive system of mountain bike trails on the East Coast. The Monongahela National Forest has a self-guiding Civil War Tour. Many of the small towns hold Civil War festivals and re-enactments throughout the year. The state Visitor Center on Route 340 in Harpers Ferry can provide you with additional information.

10 Harpers Ferry

Start:
Harpers Ferry, Jefferson County, West Virginia; Route 270 or
Route 70 to Route 340 West. Upon entering West Virginia follow
signs to Visitor Center and Parking Shuttle. Turn left at traffic
light and enter park. Admission charge includes shuttle service.

Ride(s):
5.9 Miles; Very hilly.

Hike(s):
3.0, 3.9, or 5.1 Miles; Moderate to steep climbing involved.
Trails are well marked and maintained. Options include
Maryland Heights (overlook cliffs or stone fort) and Loudoun
Heights. All trails have spectacular views and Civil War signifi-
gance. Detailed trail guides are available at the Visitor Center.

Reading:
Black Voices from Harpers Ferry, Jean Libby, (Berkeley,
California, 1979)

Perhaps no other small town in America contains as much history and scenic beauty as Harpers Ferry, West Virginia. It is sit-
uated between the Potomac and
Shenandoah Rivers and three
heights of the Blue Ridge
Mountains. Harpers Ferry's
unique geographic position
came to the attention of Robert
Harper, who established his
ferry service in 1747.

> *I, John Brown, am now quite
> certain that the crimes of this
> guilty land will never be
> purged away, but with blood. I
> had as I now think, mainly
> flattered myself that without
> very much bloodshed;
> it might be done.*
>
> John Brown, December 2, 1859

By the late 1700s, a small
town had developed around the
ferry. In the 1790s George
Washington gave the town a
boost, when he urged congress to build an armory here along
the banks of the Potomac. Congress complied and more industry
soon followed. By the middle of the 1800s, Harpers Ferry was a
prosperous town of 3,000 inhabitants.

John Brown recognized its importance and chose the town as

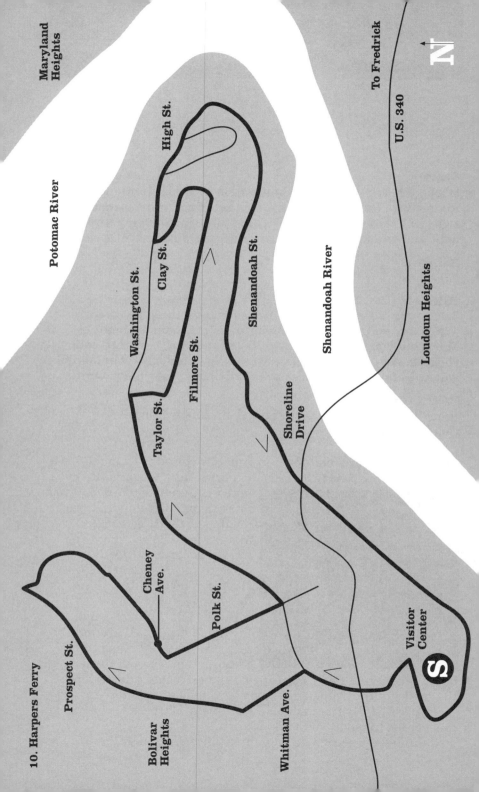

10. Harpers Ferry

This small firehouse was used by John Brown and his men as a fort during their failed attempt to seize Harpers Ferry.

the focus of his October 1859 raid. He was the first of many Civil War historical figures drawn to the town including Robert E. Lee, Jeb Stuart, Stonewall Jackson, John Wilkes Booth and Abraham Lincoln. Because of its strategic location, the town and the surrounding heights were fought over repeatedly during the war. In September 1862 the Confederates captured the town resulting in the largest U.S. Army surrender until Baatan in World War II.

The destruction caused by the war and a series of floods in the late 1800s severely crippled the town's economy. The only cheerful aspect of the town's history during this time was the establishment of Storer College. This college was a pioneer in the African-American education movement and was responsible for the education of many African-American professionals. In 1906 W.E.B. Dubois and the Second Niagara Movement met here, leading ultimately to the formation of the NAACP.

By the 1940s the National Park Service recognized the town's importance and extensive restoration work was undertaken, resulting in the 2,500 acre Harpers Ferry National Historical Park. Today it is one of the most popular tourist attractions in the Washington area. The bicycle tour, while only 5.9 miles long, connects all the historical sites in the park. If you combine the ride with one of the hikes and a walk through the shopping area in the lower town, plan on spending a full day in the park. Automobile and pedestrian traffic can be quite heavy in parts of the park during weekends from April to October. Use caution if you plan your trip during this time.

Directions:

0.0 Exit parking area toward Route 340 on Shoreline Road. Start odometer at stop sign past entrance kiosk.
Please visit the center before leaving. There is supplemental lit-

erature available and there are interpretive programs during the summer months.

0.2 Stop. Intersection with Route 340. Continue straight across the highway.

0.3 Left on Whitman Avenue (unmarked). Sign for Bolivar Heights.
At the top of the hill, on the left, is the entrance to this portion of the National Park. Bolivar Heights is the lowest (about 700 feet) of the three heights surrounding Harpers Ferry. These heights were the key to the control of Harpers Ferry. Robert E. Lee understood their importance and, upon reaching Frederick, devised a plan to effect the capture or force the retreat of the large Union garrison stationed there. He boldly divided his already outnumbered army and sent them to occupy the heights.

The Union commander at Harpers Ferry, Colonel Dixon S. Miles, was also well aware of the importance of Maryland, Loudoun and Bolivar Heights. However, for reasons attributable to alcohol or poor judgement or both, Miles failed miserably in his assignment. Maryland Heights was inadequately defended and the troops assigned there panicked and were swept off. Loudoun Heights went completely undefended and the Confederates established artillery there with no opposition.

Stonewall Jackson completed the encirclement of Harpers Ferry by occupying Schoolhouse Ridge, which is located just west of here. Outnumbered and at the mercy of Confederate artillery located on the surrounding heights, Colonel Miles was forced to surrender on September 15, 1862. One last artillery shell landed near Miles and mortally wounded him. If he was not killed he would have undoubtedly faced a court martial for this—the largest surrender of Federal troops during the war. There is a walking trail here with interpretive markers and still visible entrenchments.

1.4 Steep winding descent. Use caution. (Turns into Prospect Street, then Cheney Avenue.)

1.7 Stop. Left on Polk Street.

2.0 Stop. Left on Washington Street.
At 2.5 Miles is Stonewall Jackson's headquarters during his 1861 command of forces in the area.

2.7 Right on Taylor Street.

2.8 Stop. Left on Fillmore Street.
This is Camp Hill. This area was used for Union encampments

The tremendous view of Harpers Ferry is one of the rewards of the steep Maryland Heights hiking trail.

during the war. Before the war the large buildings were constructed for various employees of the National Armory. After the war the buildings were used by Storer College. There are a series of interpretive markers.

3.3 Steep descent and hairpin turn. Use caution.
Harper Cemetery on right. Spectacular view of Potomac River and Maryland Heights.

3.5 Stop. Right on Washington Street.
This becomes High Street as you enter the lower town. Many shops, restaurants and historical buildings are located along this street.

3.9 Stop. Right on Shenandoah Street.
The most famous building in Harpers Ferry, John Brown's Fort, is located across Shenandoah Street to the left of this intersection. Beyond this building is the footbridge over the Potomac River and access to the Chesapeake and Ohio Canal National Park. The Master Armorer's House and other historic buildings are located further along Shenandoah Street. An information center with a bookstore and public restrooms is on the right as you leave the lower town. At 4.4 Miles are the ruins of the Shenandoah Pulp Factory, one of many factories that ceased operation in the late 1800s.

4.6 Left on Shoreline Drive (follow exit and parking sign).
On left was the former site of Hall's Rifle Works, a forerunner in the factory production of armaments. Start up steep hill with the Shenandoah River on your left.

5.9 Right into parking area.

End of tour.

Start:
Shepherdstown, Jefferson County, West Virginia; Route 340 West to Boonsboro Exit. Route 67 North to end of road. Left on Main Street through Boonsboro. Left on Potomac Street (Route 34). Route 34 crosses Potomac River and enters Shepherdstown, West Virginia. Parking is available on most side streets. Start at the Old Court House (McMurran Hall) at corner of German Street and Church Street.

Ride(s):
9.5 Miles; Fairly level with one steep climb.

Hike(s):
1 Mile; Walking tour of Shepherdstown. A map describing the many historic buildings and sites is available at the Welcome Center located on King Street.

Reading:
I Rode With Stonewall, Henry Kyd Douglas, (University of North Carolina Press, Chapel Hill, N.C., 1940)

> *The wounded continued to arrive until the town was quite unable to hold all the disabled and suffering. They filled every building and overflowed into the country round, into farm houses, barns, corn cribs, cabins, wherever four walls and a roof were found together... every inch of space, and yet the cry was for more room.*

Mary Bedinger, a resident of Shepherdstown describing Shepherdstown on September 18, 1862.

Shepherdstown is located just north of a historically important Potomac River crossing. This ford has been known variously as Boteler's, Blacksford and Pack Horse. It was used by early settlers traveling from Frederick west to the Shenandoah Valley. In 1730 Thomas Shepherd recognized its importance and purchased 222 acres just north of the ford. The town is West Virginia's oldest with a charter granted on December 23, 1762 by the Virginia General Assembly.

When the Civil War started, most Shepherdstown residents

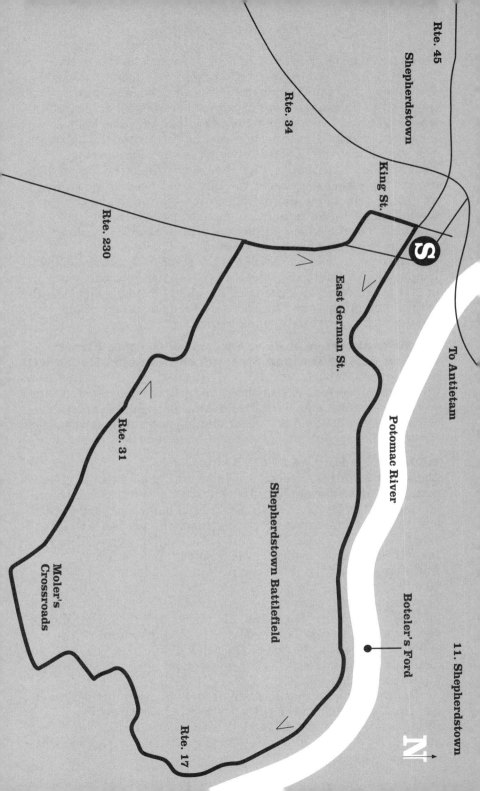

Rte. 45

Shepherdstown

Rte. 34

King St.

Rte. 230

East German St.

S

To Antietam

Potomac River

Rte. 31

Shepherdstown Battlefield

Moler's
Crossroads

Boteler's Ford

11. Shepherdstown

Rte. 17

N

were southern sympathizers and many young men joined the Confederate army. The most famous of these was Henry Kyd Douglas, who served on the staff of Stonewall Jackson. Douglas and many other Confederate soldiers from Shepherdstown returned to their hometown in September 1862 when Antietam was fought just five miles east of town. The town, as Mary Bedinger described, became one vast hospital after the battle. The ford, known as Boteler's during the war, became the Confederate retreat route after the battle. When the Union followed this retreat too closely, the Battle of Shepherdstown was fought on September 19. The Federals were convincingly repulsed and the Antietam Campaign came to a close.

This short ride gives you the opportunity to bicycle along the Potomac River and by the location of the Battle of Shepherdstown. Here you will see the steep cliffs, where many Union soldiers fell to their death. Leaving the Potomac you will pass through Molers Crossroads, the site of a small skirmish after Gettysburg. After your ride and walk take advantage of one of the fine restaurants in Shepherdstown.

0.0 Start at corner of King Street and German Street. Proceed east on German Street (The Old Court House will be on your left).
Continue on German Street through town, obeying all stops at cross streets, over the Norfolk and Southern railroad tracks. Use caution as you descend the steep winding road to the Potomac River.

1.6 Boteler's Ford and Mill Ruins.
At Boteler's Ford Confederate cavalry sentinels lined the river with flaming torches to light the way for Lee's retreating troops on the night of September 18, 1862. First came the supply wagons, then the ambulances carrying those wounded who could survive the journey south. Next, came the walking wounded and Lee's infantry and cavalry. It was a solemn procession. At Antietam, The Army of Northern Virginia had suffered over 10,000 casualties—almost one quarter of the men who had marched into Maryland two weeks previously. When the regimental bands struck up "Maryland, My Maryland" they were shouted down and told to play "Carry Me Back to Old Virginny." The going was slow and the last of the army didn't pass Lee, who was mounted on his horse Traveller midstream, until the sun was rising on September 19.

To protect his retreat Lee deployed 44 pieces of artillery and two small brigades on the cliffs overlooking the river. The Federals soon approached the Potomac and an artillery duel commenced. By dusk the Federals gained a foothold on this bank of the river and seized four of the Confederate guns. The Confederate commander of the rearguard, General William Pendleton, panicked and rode frantically toward Lee. Finding   Lee asleep he awoke him with the story that all his artillery had been seized. Lee and Stonewall Jackson decided to send back A.P. Hill's entire division the next morning to prevent further Federal attacks on their rear.

At the same time three more Federal brigades were sent across the Potomac. Two of the Federal brigades became aware of the advancing Confederates along the road to the west. However, the third brigade had climbed the cliffs north of this intersection and separated from the other Federals, and were unaware of the Confederates. This brigade, the 118th Pennsylvania, was new to the army. To make matters worse they soon found out that many of their rifles were defective. Outnumbered and trapped on the top of these cliffs, they soon fled. Many were killed or injured falling down the cliffs. Others tried to seek shelter in the archways of the Lime Kiln that is still visible on the side of the cliff. Their bad luck turned worse when a Federal battery on the other shore mistakenly opened fire on this spot. By 2 p.m. most of the fighting was over and the Confederates had driven the last Federals out of Virginia. The 118th Pennsylvania lost 269 of its 750 men.

A.P. Hill's division marched from Harpers Ferry to Antietam along this road on September 17, 1862. Hill's division was forced to march 17 miles in eight hours in order to reach Antietam in time to counter the Union surge on the Confederate right.

3.4 Road bends to right away from river. Start up steep hill.

5.5 Stop. Right on Route 31 (unmarked).

5.8 Right on Route 31 (sign for Shepherdstown).
This intersection is Molers Crossroads. A Confederate cavalry company was formed with recruits from this area. On July 15, 1863 a small skirmish was fought here between the 12th Virginia and 8th Pennsylvania.

8.5 Stop. Right on Route 230.

9.2 Road bends to left, as you enter Shepherdstown.

9.3 Straight across railroad tracks, onto Washington Street.

9.4 Stop. Right on King Street.

9.4 Stop. Straight at intersection with New Street.

9.5 Stop. Intersection of King and German Street.

End of tour.

Pennsylvania

Pennsylvania's Civil War history can be traced to 1767, the year Charles Mason and Jeremiah Dixon finished their survey of the Maryland-Pennsylvania border. With Pennsylvania's and the North's ultimate movement toward abolition, the Mason-Dixon line became the northern boundary of slavery and a powerful symbol of the upcoming conflict. Pennsylvania abolitionists and politicians were a dynamic force against the Fugitive Slave Act in the 1850s. In the 1860 election, the Pennsylvania vote helped secure Lincoln's victory.

When the war started, Pennsylvania sent the first troops to the defense of Washington. More than 300,000 troops served in the Union army and navy, including Generals McClellan, Meade, and Hancock and Admirals David Porter and John Dahlgren. In addition, Pennsylvania provided manufacturing, shipping, and agriculture to the Union cause.

The war first reached Pennsylvania in October 1862, when J.E.B. Stuart's cavalry rode around McClellan's army after the Battle of Antietam. They raided the railroad depot at Chambersburg and crossed South Mountain before returning to Maryland. The Army of Northern Virginia followed this route when they returned to Pennsylvania in June 1863. Before the Battle of Gettysburg, Lee's army reached almost as far north as Harrisburg and as far east as Wrightsville. Small engagements were fought at Carlisle and Hanover as part of the Gettysburg Campaign.

The last Confederate invasion of Pennsylvania occured on June 30, 1864. The residents of Chambersburg awoke to find their town occupied by 2,800 Confederate troops, under General John McCausland. He demanded 100,000 in gold or 500,000 in Union currency from the town leaders in retribution for Union destruction in the Shenandoah Valley. When he did not receive it, the town was put to the torch. Over 300 buildings were burned to the ground and 5,000 residents left homeless. Chambersburg became the only northern town destroyed during the war.

Of course, Pennsylvania's Civil War history is inseparable from the Battle of Gettysburg. Over 30,000 Pennsylvanians took part in the battle. The Gettysburg National Military Park contains over 35 miles of roads and 3,875 acres of well-preserved park land. Combined with the surrounding Adams County countryside, this is one of America's best areas for both Civil War exploration and recreational bicycling.

12 Gettysburg

Start:
Gettysburg, Adams County, Pennsylvania; I-270 North or I-70 West to Route 15 North. Take the Steinwehr Avenue (Emmitsburg Road–Business Route 15) Exit. Turn right at the second National Park entrance sign to Visitor Center Parking. If this lot is full, follow signs to additional parking at the Cyclorama Center.

Ride(s):
13.0, 33.4, or 34.3 Miles; Flat to very hilly.

Hike(s):
1, 3.5, or 9 Miles; Hikes start at the Cyclorama Center, Big Round Top and McMillan Woods. Trails are well-marked and maps are available from the Visitor Center. Terrain varies from smooth and flat to rocky and steep. Wear proper footwear and use caution where trails cross roadways.

Reading:
The Gettysburg Campaign: A Study in Command, Edwin B. Coddington, (Scribner's, New York, 1968)

On July 1–3, 1863 Gettysburg's quiet town, farms and woods were transformed into North America's largest battlefield. As with many great battles, Gettysburg started by chance. Wanting to divert the war from the strained Virginia countryside, Robert E. Lee had invaded Pennsylvania without a precise battle plan. The lead elements of the Army of Northern Virginia reached Chambersburg on June 24. From this point the army fanned out across the Pennsylvania countryside.

Jubal Early's division marched east toward York and Wrightsville (which contained an important bridge over the Susquehanna). On July 26 he encountered a militia force at Gettysburg and drove them from town (some scholars consider these the first shots of the Battle of Gettysburg). General Robert Rodes's division marched northeast through Carlisle toward Harrisburg. Other units marched west to forage, while Longstreet's and A.P. Hill's corps (at the rear of the long column) marched through Maryland and camped around Chambersburg.

Every Confederate
state is represented by
a monument along
Seminary Ridge.

On June 30, one of A.P. Hill's brigades, under James
Pettigrew, marched east to Gettysburg in search of shoes and
withdrew when they observed Federal cavalry approaching from
Emmitsburg. Pettigrew reported the sighting to Hill and his
division commander, Henry Heth. Hill dismissed the Federal
force as minor and gave his permission for Heth's entire division
to march the next morning and enter Gettysburg, despite Lee's
orders not to engage the enemy before the entire army was concentrated.

Hill's conclusions about the size of the Federal force were
wrong. Indeed, operating without the benefit of most of their
cavalry under Jeb Stuart, the entire Confederate army had been
unaware of the proximity of the Army of the Potomac. Under
the new leadership of General George Meade, the Union army
had paralleled the Confederate march north. Late on the night
of June 28, Lee and Longstreet were shocked to learn from a spy
named Harrison, that two Union corps were already at
Frederick, Maryland and moving north.

When Heth's division marched east on the morning of July 1
he encountered an entire Union cavalry division blocking his
entrance to town. Heth deployed his force across both sides of
the Chambersburg Pike and attacked. Although neither Lee nor
Meade had chosen Gettysburg, they were both soon rushing
more troops to the engagement and the Battle of Gettysburg
was underway. After the Confederates withdrew on July 4, the
armies had suffered over 40,000 casualties and the area was

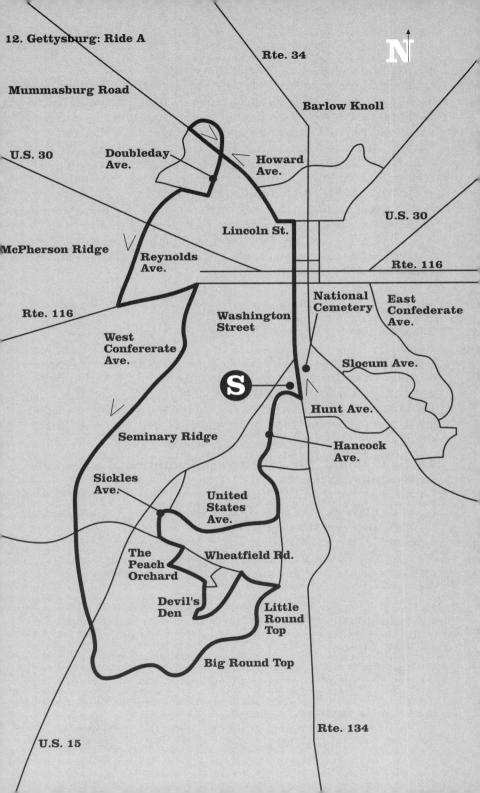

12. Gettysburg: Ride A

N

Mummasburg Road

Rte. 34

Barlow Knoll

U.S. 30

Doubleday Ave.

Howard Ave.

U.S. 30

Lincoln St.

McPherson Ridge

Rte. 116

Reynolds Ave.

Rte. 116

National Cemetery

East Confederate Ave.

Washington Street

Slocum Ave.

West Confererate Ave.

S

Hunt Ave.

Seminary Ridge

Hancock Ave.

Sickles Ave.

United States Ave.

The Peach Orchard

Wheatfield Rd.

Devil's Den

Little Round Top

Big Round Top

Rte. 134

U.S. 15

transformed into a vast hospital and cemetery. Gettysburg had entered the pantheon of American history.

These three rides focus on different aspects of this important event and vary in their difficulty. Ride A covers the main battlefield and is relatively easy. Ride B covers the rolling farmland north and east of Gettysburg and returns through the East Cavalry Battlefield and Culp's Hill. This ride is moderately difficult. Ride C heads north and west of Gettysburg, through orchards, steep hills, and small towns. It follows the Confederate approach over South Mountain, through Cashtown and along Marsh Creek to Black House Tavern. This ride is fairly difficult.

All three rides share a common start through the town of Gettysburg, and can be easily combined for a longer ride. The Visitor Center contains a number of interesting displays and is an excellent place to start your visit.

Directions: Ride A

0.0 Exit Visitor Center parking to left on Taneytown Road.
This is West Cemetery Hill, which took its name from Evergreen Cemetery. On the afternoon and evening of July 1, Union forces were driven through town and reformed their lines on this hill. During the day Brigadier General Adolph von Steinwehr posted artillery and oversaw the construction of breastworks on this small rise.

0.2 Traffic light. Straight across Steinwehr Avenue, now on Washington Street.
Continue straight on Washington Street, through a series of traffic lights and four-way stop signs. Obey all signs and use caution through town—moderate traffic.

Confederates, under Jubal Early, first entered the town on June 26 after forcing a raw Pennsylvania militia regiment to retreat. Early stayed for only a short time before marching toward York.

On June 30 soldiers, this time Union cavalry, once again entered town and headed west (left) on Chambersburg Street to probe the Confederate location. After the Union forces were driven through town the next day, Gettysburg was the location of confusion and fighting. Civilians and Union soldiers hid in cellars, churches became hospitals and Confederates went from house to house looking for food and the enemy. The Confederates occupied the town for the next three days.

There are a few notable buildings along this section of the ride. The building on the southeast corner of the intersection of

Washington Street and West High Street still contains a Whitworth cannon artillery bolt imbedded in its second story. Just east of the intersection of Washington Street and Chambersburg Street was the former home of Thaddeus Stevens, U.S. congressman and ardent abolitionist. After crossing the railroad tracks (Lincoln used this railroad to travel to Gettysburg to deliver the Gettysburg Address on November 19), Gettysburg College is on the left. The large white building visible on the left at 1.2 Miles is Pennsylvania Hall. It was used as an observation post and hospital during the battle.

1.3 Four-Way Stop. Left on Lincoln Avenue.

1.4 Right on College Avenue, which becomes Mummasburg Road.

2.3 Right on North Confederate Avenue.
Entering part of the first day battlefield, Confederate General Robert Rodes's division occupied this hill at 1 p.m. on July 1. They attacked the Union force deployed on Oak Ridge just south of here. Rodes's attack was poorly coordinated and resulted in over 2,500 casualties.

The Eternal Light Peace Memorial was dedicated in 1938 in a ceremony attended by 1,800 Civil War Veterans.

2.6 Stop. Straight across Mummasburg Road, now on Doubleday Avenue.
The Federals met the Confederate assault from Oak Hill along this ridge and behind the stone wall at the base. They stopped the Confederates for almost two hours before being forced to retreat through town.

3.2 Stop. Left on Reynolds Avenue.
At 3.4 Miles you cross over the Western Maryland Railroad. During the battle, this was an unfinished railroad cut. It was used by both armies as a defensive position during the fighting on July 1. The 149th Pennsylvania Regiment, the Bucktails, attacked an advancing Confederate brigade from this spot. The Bucktails lost over two thirds of their men holding the area around the cut.

3.4 Traffic light. Straight across Route 30 (Chambersburg Pike).
The fighting on July 1 started just west of this ridge. 2,700 Union cavalrymen, under General John Buford, dismounted and deployed along a 1,000 yard line east of Willoughby Run. They faced over 7,000 Confederates under Major General Henry Heth. They stalled the Confederate advance for two hours, while waiting for infantry reinforcements under General John Reynolds.

The Colonel William Wells Monument near Big Round Top. Wells was awarded the Congressional Medal of Honor for his heroism at Gettysburg.

Reynold's and the 1st Division of the I Corps of the Army of the Potomac reached the field at 10 a.m. As they started to fill the forward ranks, Reynolds was killed by a skirmisher's bullet to the head. However, their arrival turned the tide and most Confederates were forced to fall back west of Willoughby Run.

By 11 a.m. the battle quieted as both sides rushed reinforcements to the field. In the early afternoon both armies had expanded their lines in an arc north and south of this ridge. The fighting resumed and, with tremendous losses on both sides, the Confederates gained the field by late afternoon. With the collapse of the Union defense, southern success might have been assured if Richard Ewell, who had replaced Stonewall Jackson, had pressed the attack on Cemetery Hill. However, Ewell lacked Jackson's aggressiveness and the Federals were allowed to strengthen their defenses during the night of July 1.

4.2 Stop. Left on Route 116 (Fairfield Road).

4.7 Traffic light. Right on West Confederate Avenue.
The Lutheran Theological Seminary is to the left at this intersection. The cupola of its main building was used by both armies as an observation post.

West Confederate Avenue follows Seminary Ridge, the main

Devil's Den at the base of Little Round Top.

Confederate position on July 2 and 3. There are numerous monuments and interpretive markers along this road. Pickett's Charge occurred on July 3 in the fields in front of the Virginia Memorial. On July 2 the left of Longstreet's line was anchored at the current location of the Mississippi Monument. Barksdale's brigade attacked the Federals in the Peach Orchard from this spot. An observing Federal colonel recalled it was "the grandest charge that was ever made by mortal man."

6.7 Four-way stop. Straight through intersection with Millerstown Road, still on West Confederate Avenue.
The Confederate attack on the Wheatfield was launched from here by Kershaw's brigade on July 2.

7.4 Stop. Cross Emmitsburg Road, now on South Confederate Avenue.
Where the road bends to the left is Warfield Ridge. The Confederate right was anchored here on July 2. The Confederate attack on Devil's Den, the Wheatfield and the Round Tops was launched from here.

Shift gears as you start up the edge of Big Round Top. At 8.8 Miles is access to the Big Round Top Loop Trail. Colonel William C. Oates's regiment reached the summit after facing fire from "behind the rocks and crags which covered the side of the mountain thicker than gravestones in a city cemetery," Oates later recalled. Although Oates wanted to hold Big Round Top and place artillery here, he was ordered to attack Little Round Top.

His regiment swept down the northeastern slope of Big Round

Top and across the low spot before Little Round Top without encountering any resistance. However, as they started to ascend the southeast slope of Little Round Top, they were met with strong resistance from the 20th Maine. This regiment, under Colonel Joshua Chamberlain, was the absolute left of the Army of the Potomac. In one of the war's more memorable fights, Chamberlain's regiment repulsed the Confederates with a bayonet charge and secured Little Round Top. There is a short footpath to the 20th Maine Monument on the right side of the road at the summit.

9.4 Little Round Top Summit.
Meade's chief engineer, General Gouverneur Warren, discovered this important hill was unoccupied by either army on July 2. He ordered infantry regiments to occupy the hill and they arrived just minutes before the attacking Confederates. There are monuments and interpretive markers identifying the various landmarks visible from the summit. Use caution on the short steep descent.

9.4 Stop. Left on Wheatfield Road.

9.7 Left on Crawford Avenue. Walk bicycle across cattle guards at both ends of this road.
This area of large boulders became known as the Valley of Death. Confederates reached Plum Run and the lower slope of Little Round Top, before being repulsed.

Devil's Den is on your right after crossing the second cattle guard. After fierce fighting, Confederates controlled Devil's Den on the afternoon of July 2. Sharpshooters plagued Union artillerymen posted on Little Round Top from this small "fort".

Shift gears as you climb the steep twisting road to the top of the Devil's Den. Follow the road as it curves to the right, past the intersection with Ayres Avenue. At 10.5 Miles is the Wheatfield. Some of the battle's most concentrated fighting took place across this field.

10.9 Left on Wheatfield Road.

11.1 Right on Sickles Avenue.
On July 2, Union General Daniel Sickles' III Corps occupied the Peach Orchard which was located on this low ridge. His position was far in front of the main Union line along Cemetery Ridge and vulnerable to attack. When the attack came, the III Corps was forced to fall back to the ridge.

11.3 Stop. Right on United States Avenue.

12.0 Stop. Left on Hancock Avenue.

This is the lowest section of Cemetery Ridge. As Union troops were shifted south to block the Confederate attack on Little Round Top, the Wheatfield, and the Peach Orchard, a gap was left in this section of the ridge on July 2. General Winfield Scott Hancock observed the gap and an advancing Confederate brigade. Fearing disaster, Hancock ordered the 1st Minnesota Regiment to block the Confederate advance. The 1st Minnesota succeeded in forcing the Confederates back, but only 47 men of the original 262 remained fit for duty after the charge. This was the highest Union regimental loss of the war. The Pennsylvania Memorial, the park's largest, is located further along the ridge. At 12.8 Miles is The Angle and Copse of Trees.

At this location the Battle of Gettysburg came to its climax. The center of the Union line was the focus of Pickett's charge on the afternoon of July 3. Hand to hand fighting ensued as some of the 12,000 Confederates survived the bombardment and exposed mile long march across the fields to the left (west) and reached this location. Eventually, all were killed, wounded, forced to retreat or taken prisoner.

13.0 Stop. Right on cyclorama parking road. Take walkway to Visitor Center on left.

End of tour.

Directions: Ride B

(Follow directions for Ride A to 1.4 Miles.)

1.6 Right on Howard Avenue (Unmarked, it is the first road past tennis courts and Gettysburg College athletic fields).

2.0 Stop. Straight across Carlisle Road (Route 34), still on Howard Avenue.

General Francis Barlow's division occupied this hill on July 1. They were attacked by Early's corps from the north and east. They were outnumbered and outflanked and soon fled south toward town. Barlow was found seriously wounded by Confederate General John Brown Gordon, who ordered several nearby soldiers to place Barlow on a litter and carry him to shade. As Gordon continued toward town, he was certain Barlow would soon die from his wound. Barlow survived and later in the war learned of the death of a Confederate General named J.B. Gordon in a fight near Richmond. Of course, Barlow assumed he was the same Gordon who had showed him some kindness at Gettysburg. However, the dead General was Gordon's relative James Byron Gordon.

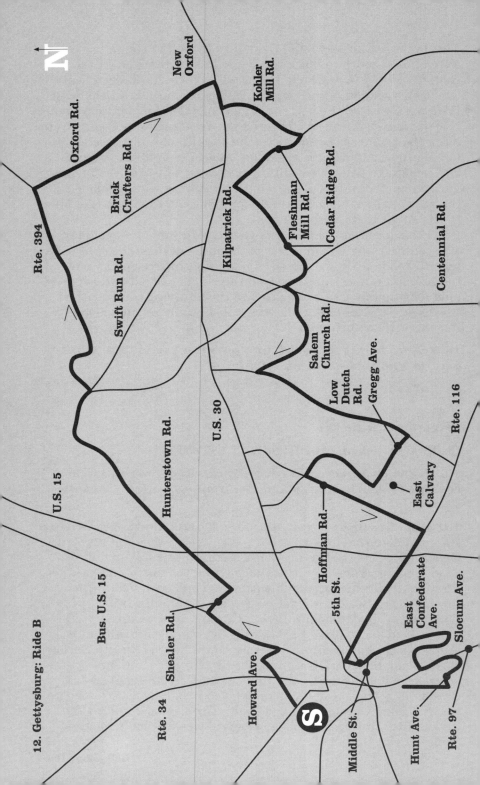

12. Gettysburg: Ride B

N

Oxford Rd.

New Oxford

Kohler Mill Rd.

Rte. 394

Brick Crafters Rd.

Kilpatrick Rd.

Fleshman Mill Rd.

Cedar Ridge Rd.

Centennial Rd.

Swift Run Rd.

Salem Church Rd.

Gregg Ave.

Low Dutch Rd.

Hunterstown Rd.

U.S. 30

Rte. 116

U.S. 15

East Calvary

Hoffman Rd.

Bus. U.S. 15

5th St.

Shealer Rd.

Rte. 34

East Confederate Ave.

Howard Ave.

Slocum Ave.

Middle St.

S

Hunt Ave.

Rte. 97

Cress's Ridge at the East Cavalry Battlefield Site. Jeb Stuart launched his unsuccessful cavalry charge across these fields.

When Gordon was serving in the U.S. Senate almost fifteen years after the war the two met again at a dinner. Gordon wrote, "Nothing short of resurrection from the dead could have amazed either of us more." The two remained good friends until Barlow's death in 1896. This small hill is now called Barlow's Knoll in his honor.

2.5 Stop. Left on Old Harrisburg Road (Business Route 15).
Early's force attacked down this road.

3.5 Right on Shealer Road.

4.0 Stop. Left on Hunterstown Road.

7.2 Stop. Right on Shrivers Corner Road (Route 394).
This is one of the oldest roads in the county and was used by Confederates on their march from York to Gettysburg on July 1.

7.9 Left on Route 394 (Hampton Road). Use caution.

11.5 Stop. Right on Oxford Road.
Many of these buildings in New Chester were built in the 18th century.

15.1 Yield, go one quarter around the circle in New Oxford onto Route 30 West.
Confederates, under Jubal Early, marched through New Oxford on June 26 and 27. There are a few restaurants and stores in town and it is a good place to take a break. New Oxford was laid out in 1792 and today is known as the "Little Town with the Beautiful Circle."

The Confederates took advantage of this rich Pennsylvania Dutch countryside. While the Confederate army was under orders not to pillage or destroy private property, they seized food, livestock, and clothing in exchange for worthless Confederate IOUs and script. In addition, in one of the war's cruelest episodes, dozens of black Pennsylvanians were seized by the Confederates and sold into slavery.

15.5 Left on Kohler Mill Road.

16.6 Stop. Right on Fleshman Mill Road.
Cross bridge over Conewago Creek and bear right as you get to the top of the hill.

17.3 Stop. Straight across Bon-Ox Road.

17.8 Left on Cedar Ridge Road.

19.5 Stop. Right on Centennial Road.

19.9 Left on Kilpatrick Road.

20.2 Right on Salem Church Road.

21.8 Stop. Left on Low Dutch Road.
Salem Church was built originally in 1856 and rebuilt in 1888 and 1904.

22.5 Stop. Straight across Granite Station Road, still on Low Dutch Road.

24.0 Right on Gregg Avenue (sign for East Cavalry Field faces the opposite direction).
On July 3, Jeb Stuart attempted an attack on the Union rear in conjunction with Pickett's charge on the Union center. Stuart's 6,300 cavalrymen occupied Cress's Ridge, which is located one mile to the northwest of this intersection. Union cavalry, under General David Gregg, were positioned along the Hanover Road, a half mile south of this intersection.

Shortly after noon, Stuart deployed his men and a series of charges and counter-charges took place on this open plain. At the height of the battle George Custer led the 1st Michigan headlong into the front of the charging Confederates. In the collision horses were flipped end over end and their riders were crushed. The countercharges by the Federals stopped the Confederate attack and both sides returned to their original positions. Although the Union suffered more casualties (254 to 181), they had prevented Stuart from affecting the outcome of the main battle on Cemetery Ridge.

This road parallels the center of this well-preserved battlefield and then turns sharply to follow Cress's Ridge. There are monuments and interpretive markers on both sides of this narrow road.

25.9 Stop. Left on Hoffman Road.

27.5 Stop. Right on Hanover Road (Route 116).
Use caution, there is moderate traffic on this road. Watch for merging traffic at the Route 15 overpass. After the overpass, you climb a small steep hill. This is Benner's Hill which the Confederates used to bombard Union positions at Culp's Hill.

29.5 Left on Fifth Street.
Re-enter town of Gettysburg.

29.5 Stop. Right on Middle Street.
The Culp farmhouse, which was used as a hospital after the battle, is on the left.

29.8 Left on Liberty Street (East Confederate Avenue).
Bear left at the school and enter the National Park. As the road enters the woods, it follows Confederate positions on July 2 and 3 at the base of Culp's Hill. There are monuments on the left side of the road. This is the hook end of the "fishook" position of both armies.

31.2 Stop. Right on Slocum Avenue.
Spangler's Spring is at this intersection. Shift gears as you start up Culp's Hill to the right.

31.7 Stop. Left, still on Slocum Avenue.
There is an observation tower .2 Mile to the right at this intersection.

32.2 Left, still on Slocum Avenue (Wainwright Avenue is straight).
East Cemetery Hill runs north of this intersection. Confederates were unsuccessful in their attempt to seize this hill on the evening of July 2.

32.3 Stop. Left on Baltimore Street (Route 97).
The Spangler home, which was used as a hospital, is on the left as you descend Cemetery Hill.

The Sachs Mill Covered Bridge was built in the 1840s.

32.7 Right on Hunt Avenue.

33.1 Stop. Right on Taneytown Road.
General Meade's Headquarters is located across Taneytown Road at this intersection.

33.4 Left at Visitor Center entrance.

End of tour.

Directions: Ride C

(Follow directions for Ride B to 2.0 Miles).

2.0 Stop. Left on Carlisle Street (Route 34).

2.3 Right on Table Rock Road.
At 4.1 Miles on the left is the Jacob Kent farm, which was used as a hospital after the battle.

5.5 Stop. Straight across Goldenville Road.

6.7 Stop. Straight, now on Route 394 West.

8.8 Stop. Straight across Route 34 (Main Street), still on Route 394 West.
This is downtown Biglerville, known as "Apple Capital U.S.A." Biglerville was originally named Middletown. After reaching Carlisle, members of Ewell's Corps passed through Biglerville on their way to Gettysburg. There are some stores and restaurants along Main Street. The Apple Museum is past the intersection on the left.

9.2 Stop. Left on Route 234.
You are now entering one of the most productive fruit-growing areas in the Eastern United States.

10.4 Three Way Stop. Straight on Hecklenluber Road.

11.9 Stop. Straight on Excellsior Road.

12.0 Left on Fairground Road.

12.7 Stop. Right on Narrows Road.
This section of Conewago Creek, which rushes down the side of South Mountain, is known as the Narrows. It is one of the most beautiful areas of Adams County.

15.4 Left on Bottom Road.
About 1.5 miles of this road is unpaved. The road crosses Conewago Creek through this heavily wooded area. Piney Mountain Summit (1350 feet) is to the right.

18.0 Stop. Bottom Road Ends. Left on New Road (unmarked).
Shift gears as you climb the hill. Use caution as you descend the steep hill on this winding road.

20.9 Stop. Right on Cashtown Road.
Just to the left of this intersection is a unique round barn.

21.0 Bear left, still on Cashtown Road.

21.3 Stop. Straight across Route 30, now on High Street.
This is Cashtown. The first Confederates reached Cashtown on June 26, after crossing South Mountain from Chambersburg. Robert E. Lee reached Cashtown on the morning of July 1 and heard the sounds of the battle already in progress. There is an excellent view of both Little and Big Round Top from this ridge.

22.0 Stop. Left on Old Route 30.
This was the route over South Mountain during the war. Cashtown Inn is to the right of this intersection. It was featured in the filming of *Gettysburg*. The Confederate ambulances recrossed South Mountain here after the battle.

22.1 Right on Ortanna Road.

23.1 Three Way Stop. Left on Ortanna Road.

24.7 Left on Knoxlyn-Ortanna Road.
There is a wonderful view at the top of this very steep hill. Bear left as the road descends the hill.

27.2 Left on Knox Road.
Use caution crossing one lane bridge at intersection.

28.6 Right on Black Horse Tavern Road.
Marsh Creek is on the right and Herr's Ridge is on the left. On July 2 Lee ordered James Longstreet's corps to occupy a position south of Gettysburg, astride the Emmitsburg Road. In order to remain concealed from Federal observation, Longstreet's troops marched west from Herr's Tavern to Seven Stars and then followed this road behind Herr's Ridge.

30.3 Stop. Left on Route 116 (Fairfield Road).
Black Horse Tavern is on the left. There are interpretive markers in front of this historic building (private residence).

30.3 Right on Black Horse Tavern Road.
Longstreet's corps continued along this road for a few hundred yards, when Brigadier General Joseph Kershaw (in command of the lead brigade) realized the road started to ascend the southern terminus of Herr's Ridge. Kershaw realized that if they continued, they would be seen by the enemy. Kershaw halted the column and conferred with Longstreet.

Longstreet became furious and realized he would have to send his entire column back along Black Horse Tavern Road. From that point they recrossed Herr's Ridge and marched east on Route 116 (then called Hagerstown Road) to Willoughby Run Road. This route took advantage of the cover afforded by Seminary Ridge but cost Longstreet over two hours and delayed Lee's entire plan on July 2. Willoughby Run Road intersects with Black Horse Tavern Road on the left.

32.0 Stop. Left on Millerstown Road.
If you want to visit the Sachs Mill Covered Bridge turn right at this intersection (Pumping Station Road). Continue .8 mile to Scott Road and turn left to bridge. This unique bridge (note the lattice construction) is over 150 years old. Return to Pumping Station Road and continue tour.

Millerstown Road goes through the Eisenhower National Historic Site. To visit you must take a shuttle bus from the National Park Visitor Center.

32.6 Four Way Stop. Straight at intersection with West Confederate Avenue.
(This intersection joins Ride A at 6.7 Miles. You can turn right on West Confederate Avenue and follow directions from this point. It will add 6.3 miles to the tour for a total of 38.9 Miles.)

32.9 Stop. Left on Emmitsburg Road (Route 15). Use caution—moderate traffic.
Seminary Ridge and the center of the Confederate line on July 2

and 3 is on the left. Cemetery Ridge and the center of the Union line is on the right as you ride north on this road. Pickett's charge swept across this road on July 3.

34.3 Right at sign for National Park Visitor Center.

End of tour.

The Gettysburg Address

Four score and seven years ago our fathers brought forth on this continent, a new nation, conceived in Liberty, and dedicated to the proposition that all men are created equal.

Now we are engaged in a great civil war, testing whether that nation, or any nation so conceived and so dedicated, can long endure. We are met on a great battlefield of that war. We have come to dedicate a portion of that field, as a final resting place for those who here gave their lives that that nation might live. It is altogether fitting and proper that we should do this.

But, in a larger sense, we can not dedicate–we can not consecrate–we can not hallow–this ground. The brave men, living and dead, who struggled here, have consecrated it, far above our poor power to add or detract. The world will little note, nor long remember what we say here, but it can never forget what they did here. It is for us the living, rather, to be dedicated here to the unfinished work which they who fought here have thus far so nobly advanced. It is rather for us to be here dedicated to the great task remaining before us–that from these honored dead we take increased devotion to that cause for which they gave the last full measure of devotion–that we here highly resolve that these dead shall not have died in vain–that this nation, under God, shall have a new birth of freedom–and that government of the people, by the people, for the people, shall not perish from the earth.

Abraham Lincoln, November 19, 1863

Virginia

When Virginia seceded from the Union on April 17, 1861, its location and economic status made it inevitable that Virginia would become the location of much of the war. Virginia adjoined four northern and border states and Washington, D.C. Virginia contained the largest Confederate population (1,200,000 in the 1860 census) and the largest concentration of industry. When the capital of the Confederacy was moved to Richmond in May 1861, it became a logical attack point for Union armies. From First Manassas to Appomattox Court House, over half of all Civil War battles were fought in Virginia.

Virginia, home of presidents, would become home of the Civil War generals. Robert E. Lee, Stonewall Jackson, J.E.B. Stuart, A.P. Hill, and Jubal Early all came from Virginia. Virginia also supplied more soldiers and supplies to the war than any other Confederate state. Though they were neither the first to secede nor the most committed to slavery, most Virginians were willing to fight to defend their homes and their state's honor. They would pay dearly for their beliefs and armed struggle. Fredericksburg, Richmond and Petersburg were almost completely destroyed. The Shenandoah Valley was transformed from one of the world's greatest agricultural regions to an area of hunger and deprivation. Thousands of Virginians gave their lives to the lost cause of defending their state and the barbaric institution of slavery.

Virginia has several distinct geographic and economic areas. I have included tours in four of these regions: the Shenandoah Valley, Northern Virginia, the Tidewater and Central Virginia. Each offers a distinctly different geographic and Civil War experience. The Shenandoah Valley remains an area of small towns and agriculture nestled between the Blue Ridge and Allegheny Mountains. Northern Virginia is an area of rolling hills, large estates and horse farms. The Tidewater contains the expertly restored towns of Williamsburg, Yorktown, and Jamestown which are rich in Colonial as well as Civil War history. Finally, Central Virginia is a blend of mountains, rolling hills, small towns and true southern cities. Bicycling in any of these regions is a rewarding experience.

13 Winchester

Start:
Winchester, Frederick County, Virginia; Route 66 West to Exit 300 (Route 81 North). Exit 313 (Millwood Avenue West). Right on Pleasant Valley Avenue to Abrams Delight and Chamber of Commerce Visitor Center on right.

Ride(s):
26.2 or 56.9 Miles; Moderate to very hilly.

Hike(s):
1 Mile; Walking tour of downtown Winchester. Start at Kurtz Cultural Center at Boscawen and Kent streets. Historic buildings include Stonewall Jackson's Headquarters, the Frederick County Courthouse and General Sheridan's Headquarters.

Reading:
Make Me a Map of the Valley: The Civil War Journal of Stonewall Jackson's Topographer, Jedekiah Hotchkiss, Ed. by Archie P. McDonald, (Southern Methodist University Press, 1973)

As the most important town at the northern, or lower, end of the Shenandoah Valley, Winchester became a focal point of the Civil War. During the war, five battles were fought within five miles of the center of town. The town itself changed hands over 70 times during the course of the war. Citizens were subjected to many deprivations. Suspected spies were imprisoned by both armies, while their homes were burned in retaliation. Houses were turned into hospitals and military headquarters and fighting sometimes raged through the streets.

> *I do not remember having ever seen such rejoicing. Our entrance into Winchester was one of the most stirring scenes of my life*
>
> Thomas "Stonewall" Jackson in a letter to his wife, after his victory at first Winchester on May 25, 1862.

Recognizing the importance of the Shenandoah Valley and Winchester, the Confederate command ordered Stonewall Jackson to take charge of the small, ill-equipped, undisciplined

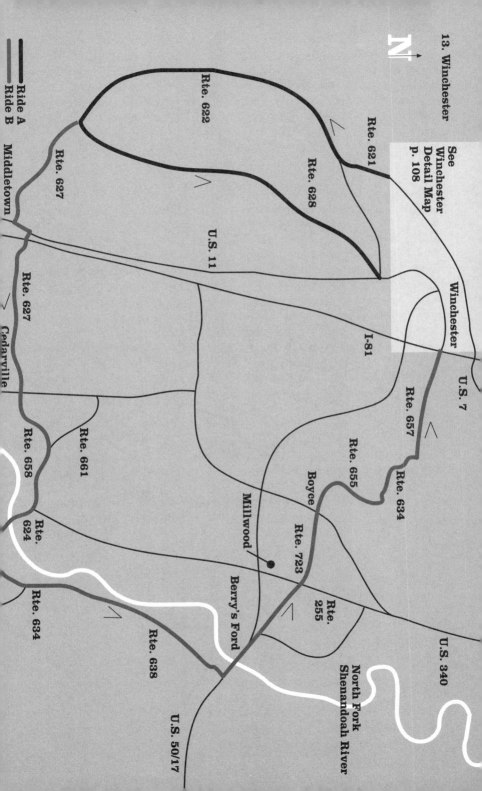

N

13. Winchester

See
Winchester
Detail Map
p. 108

Winchester

U.S. 7

Rte. 621

Rte. 628

Rte. 622

Rte. 627

Middletown

U.S. 11

I-81

Rte. 657

Rte. 634

Rte. 655

Boyce

Rte. 723

Rte.
255

Rte. 627

Cedarville

Rte. 661

Rte. 658

Rte.
624

Millwood

Berry's Ford

Rte. 634

Rte. 638

U.S. 50/17

U.S. 340

North Fork
Shenandoah River

━━ Ride A
━━ Ride B

13. Winchester: Detail

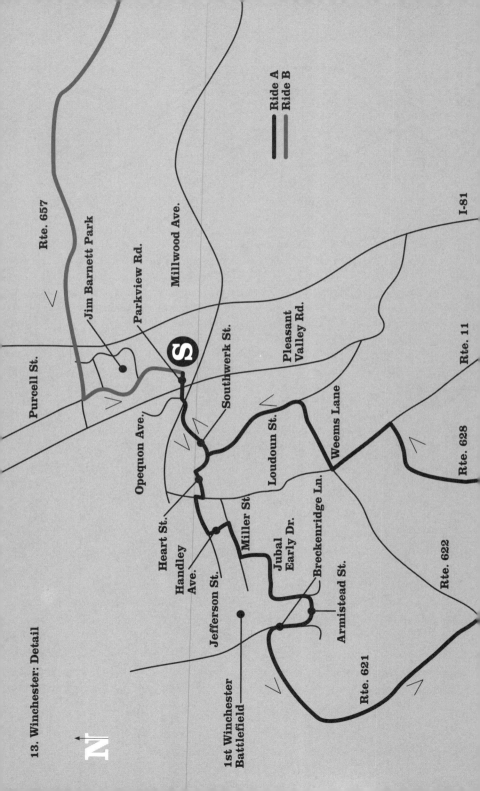

N

Rte. 657

Jim Barnett Park

Parkview Rd.

Millwood Ave.

Purcell St.

Opequon Ave.

S

Southwerk St.

Pleasant
Valley Rd.

Loudoun St.

Weems Lane

I-81

Rte. 11

Rte. 628

Heart St.

Handley
Ave.

Miller St.

Jubal
Early Dr.

Breckenridge Ln.

Armistead St.

Jefferson St.

Rte. 622

1st Winchester
Battlefield

Rte. 621

Ride A
Ride B

force located there. He arrived in Winchester on November 5, 1861 and immediately set about transforming his army. When Federal forces advanced on Winchester in March 1862, Jackson's outnumbered force withdrew south. However, Jackson had no intention of letting the Union control the Valley. On March 23 Jackson marched north and struck the Federals at Kernstown, four miles south of Winchester. While Jackson was defeated, he succeeded in forcing the Federals to keep a force in the Shenandoah Valley. Thus, the Federals were deprived of much needed reinforcements for their attack on Richmond. During the next ten weeks, Jackson would display an audacity rarely rivaled in modern warfare. Using a superior knowledge of the terrain, Jackson was able to quickly maneuver his force from one end of the Valley to the other. Striking quickly, his army defeated larger Union forces at Mcdowell, Front Royal, Winchester, and Cross Keys/Port Republic. While Jackson's command was not flawless, his campaign would become a textbook for future military commanders.

These rides connect some of the most important sites of this campaign. Because the rides start near downtown Winchester, the directions leaving town are a little complicated and there is moderate traffic. However, within three miles, you will be pedalling along some of the most beautiful, unpopulated roads in Virginia. The first week in May is an ideal time for this visit because of the Shenandoah Apple Blossom Festival.

Directions: Ride A

0.0 Exit parking by crossing Pleasant Valley Road, straight on Parkview Avenue.
Start your tour at the Visitor Center. They have many pamphlets, maps, and guidebooks available to make your visit more enjoyable. The Visitor Center is housed within an 1833 mill house. The house across the parking lot is the Abram's Delight Museum. Isaac Hollingsworth built the house from native limestone in 1754. The museum is open from April through October from 9:00 a.m.–5:00 p.m. Picnic areas and public restrooms are located here.

This park is located on the southeast corner of Winchester and next to the Millwood-Front Royal Road. Part of the First Battle of Winchester took place here on May 25, 1862. Confederate General Richard Ewell's division attacked Union Colonel Donnelly's brigade from this spot. The Federals occupied a spot just north of here. They retreated through town after a few hours of heavy fighting.

0.2 Stop. Left on Opeguon Avenue.

0.2 Stop. Right on Millwood Avenue.

0.4 Left on Southwerk Street.
Shift gears as you head up this short, steep hill.

0.6 Traffic light. Right on Loudoun Street.

0.6 Left on Hart Street.

0.7 Stop. Right on Route 11 North.

0.7 Left on Jefferson Street.
The second part of the First Battle of Winchester took place in this area. After being forced north from Front Royal and Strasburg, the Federals formed a defensive line in southern Winchester. The most important part of that line was anchored on these small hills. Stonewall Jackson attacked this line from the south and west. Eventually the attack from the west broke the Federal line and they were forced to retreat into Maryland. The area now occupied by the high school on your right was the center of the Union line.

1.1 Left on Handley Avenue (small traffic circle).

1.1 Stop. Right on Miller Street.

1.8 Stop. Left on Jubal Early Drive.
(The only reminder of the Civil War in this new development are the street names.)

1.9 Right on Armistead Street.

2.1 Yield. Right on Breckenridge Lane.

2.5 Stop. Left on Merrimans Lane (Route 621).

4.6 Stop. Right on Cedar Creek Grade (Route 622).
The First Battle of Kernstown took place just southwest of this intersection on March 23, 1862. The ridge to the left was the location of the heaviest fighting. Jackson's leadership here was flawed and Union General Shields could claim he was the only commander ever to force Jackson from a battlefield. The Federals were able to deploy their troops with greater skill and after suffering 718 casualties, Jackson was forced to retreat to Newtown (present day Stephens City).

The Second Battle of Kernstown took place on July 24, 1864 on the same basic battlefield. This time, the Confederates, under Jubal Early, were successful in dislodging the Federals. Before retreating into Maryland, the Federals sustained 1,200 casualties.

13.1 Stop. Left on Route 628 (Middle Road).
This area of small towns and fruit orchards has changed little since the Civil War. From 22 to 24 Miles, the Kernstown Battlefield is now on your left. During the first battle, Federal troops crossed the road to counter the Confederate attack on their right flank. The large hill you climb just before the next intersection is Pritchard's Hill. This was an important Union artillery position.

24.1 Traffic light. Left on Route 11 (moderate traffic).

24.1 Traffic light. Right on Weems Lane.

24.6 Traffic light. Left on Papermill Road. Becomes Loudoun Street.

25.6 Traffic light. Right on Southwerk Street.

25.8 Stop. Right on Millwood Avenue.

26.0 Left on Opequon Avenue.

26.0 Right on Parkview Avenue.

26.1 Stop. Straight across Pleasant Valley Road.

26.2 Parking.

End of tour.

Directions: Ride B

(Follow directions for Ride A to Mile 13.1).

13.1 Stop. Right on Route 622-628.

13.3 Left on Minebank Road (Route 622).

13.9 Left on Chapel Road (Route 627).
Use caution crossing railroad tracks at 17.8 Miles.

18.1 Traffic light. Left on Route 11 North.
Middletown has a few stores and restaurants and is a good place to take a break during this long ride.

This crossroads was the location of heavy fighting on May 24, 1862. Stonewall Jackson surprised the Federal garrison at Front Royal on May 23 and caused the main Union force at Strasburg to retreat north. Jackson attempted to cut off their retreat by marching northeast from Front Royal to Middletown. His artillery was able to shell the retreating Federals from a hill east of this spot. The Confederates were able to cause tremendous damage. Henry Kyd Douglas, Jackson's aide, described the destruction as "... a sickening sight, the worst I had ever seen."

However, most Federals escaped and Jackson had to continue the fight at Winchester the next day.

If you want to visit the Cedar Creek Battlefield (October 19, 1864) turn right at this intersection and ride 1.5 miles to the entrance on the right of Route 11. (See the Strasburg section for historical annotation.)

18.5 Right on Route 627.
This road was used by Jackson's forces to intercept the Federals at Middletown.

24.9 Stop. Left on Route 522-340. (Use caution.)
John S. Mosby led an attack on a Federal picket force from this point on May 21, 1864.

25.0 Right on Route 658 (Rockland Road).

27.9 Right on Route 661.

29.1 Stop. Right on Route 624.
Use caution crossing one-lane bridge over the Shenandoah River at 30.4 Miles.

30.8 Left on Route 643, becomes Route 603.

34.4 Stop. Left on Route 638.

40.7 Stop. Left on Route 50-17.
Use caution crossing bridge over Shenandoah River and riding on this brief section of Route 50. During the war, this narrow section of the river, called Berry's Ford, was used by John S. Mosby's men to raid Federal outposts in the Shenandoah Valley.

41.5 Right on Route 723 and Route 621, bear left on 723.
On December 15, 1864 Mosby's men ambushed a Federal patrol riding east on this road. They hid in the woods to your right at 43 Miles and swept down on the surprised Federals. They succeeded in capturing a number of horses and took 68 Federals prisoner.

43.8 Straight across Route 255, still on Route 723.
This small crossroads is Millwood. The large house south of this intersection was the Clarke Hotel during the war. After Lee surrendered at Appomattox, the Union commander in the area, General George Chapman, sought a meeting with John S. Mosby. The two leaders arranged a truce and met at this location on April 18 and April 20, 1865 to discuss whether Mosby would also surrender. Mosby declined to surrender, but on April 21 disbanded his command in nearby Salem. The Burwell-Morgan Mill Museum is also located in Millwood, it is open May through October, Wednesday through Sunday.

45.8 Stop. Straight across Route 340, still on Route 723.

48.3 Right on Route 655.

50.7 Straight on Route 634.

51.3 Stop. Left on Route 657.

56.0 Traffic light. Left on Purcell Street.
Enter Jim Barnett City of Winchester Park. Stay to the right.

56.9 Stop. Cross over University Drive to footbridge over Abrams Creek and parking lot.

End of tour.

14 Strasburg

Start:
Strasburg, Warren County, Virginia; I-66 West to Exit 1 (Route 81 South). Go two miles to Exit 298 (Route 11 South). Turn right at first traffic light at intersection of Route 11 and King Street (Route 55). All day parking is available on many side streets or at Strasburg High School (two blocks south of King Street on Holliday Street).

Ride(s):
20.4 or 56.8 Miles; Very hilly.

Hike(s):
2 Miles; Hilly. The Fisher's Hill battlefield is owned and operated by The Association for the Preservation of Civil War Sites. They have developed the site in partnership with the Strasburg Guards Camp. Directions to the site are included in the Ride B instructions. A detailed map is available at the site.

Reading:
The Personal Memoirs of Philip H. Sheridan, P.H. Sheridan, (New York, 1888)

On August 7, 1864 General Grant made one of his most important decisions as commander of Union armies. He appointed 33-year-old General Philip Sheridan to command the newly formed Army of the Shenandoah. Grant's decision had been prompted by the success of Confederate General Jubal Early. "Old Jube" had invaded Maryland, threatened Washington, D.C., and cavalry under his command burned Chambersburg, Pennsylvania to the ground.

> *The terrible grumble, and rumble, and roar,*
> *Telling the battle was on once more,*
> *And Sheridan twenty miles away.*
>
> Thomas Buchanan Read, Sheridan's Ride

Although Grant had succeeded in trapping Lee and the Army of Northern Virginia at Petersburg and Richmond, Early's army continued to outmaneuver four different Union commands and controlled the entire Shenandoah Valley.

This embarrassment could not only prolong the war, but

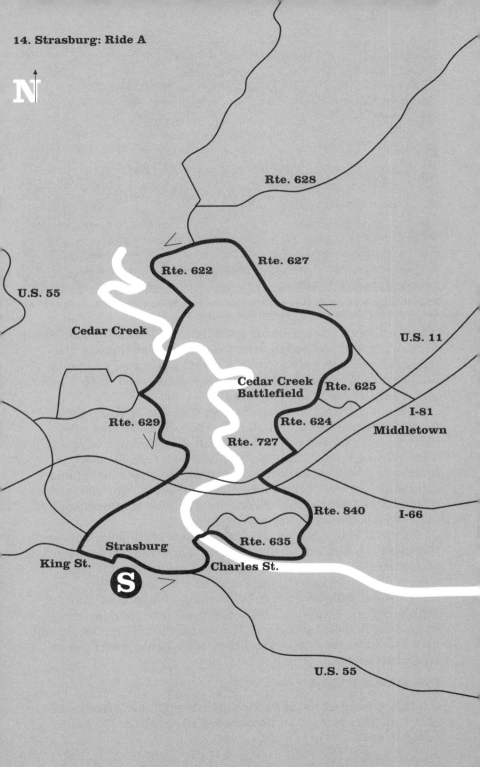

N

Rte. 628

Rte. 627

Rte. 622

U.S. 55

Cedar Creek

U.S. 11

Cedar Creek
Battlefield

Rte. 625

Rte. 629

Rte. 624

I-81
Middletown

Rte. 727

Rte. 840

I-66

Strasburg

Rte. 635

King St.

Charles St.

S

U.S. 55

Fighting took place in these fields and around Belle Grove Mansion during the Battle of Cedar Creek on October 17, 1864.

could influence the upcoming presidential election. Lincoln faced former General McClellan, who was running on a peace platform. If Early continued to elude Union forces and endanger northern cities, perhaps the electorate would turn to McClellan and a negotiated end of the war.

Sheridan proved to be the perfect choice to counter Early. From September 19 to October 19, 1864, Sheridan defeated Early in a series of four battles (Third Winchester, Fisher's Hill, Tom's Brook, and Cedar Creek). After Cedar Creek, Early's army was forced to withdraw all the way to New Market and relinquish control of the Valley to the Federals. Sheridan accomplished, in a few months, what a dozen Union commanders had failed to accomplish in three years.

The first ride explores the Cedar Creek battlefield. Some of the ride is on dirt roads, so a mountain or cross terrain bicycle is recommended. The second, longer ride winds through the George Washington National Forest and returns to the Shenandoah Valley with a difficult climb and descent over Edinburg Gap. This ride is recommended for experienced bicyclists only. Before finishing at Strasburg, the ride passes through many small historic towns and the Tom's Brook and Fisher's Hill battlefields.

Directions: Ride A

0.0 Start tour at intersection of King Street (Route 55) and Holliday Street in downtown Strasburg. Go east on King Street.

0.2 Traffic light. Straight through intersection with Route 11, now on Route 55.

0.7 Left on Charles Street (the last road before Route 55 bends sharply to the right).

0.8 Stop. Right on East Washington Street (Route 635).

2.0 Use caution crossing narrow bridge over Cedar Creek at bottom of hill. Road becomes dirt.

After being defeated at Third Winchester and Fisher's Hill, Early withdrew and Sheridan followed south to Harrisonburg. Sheridan assumed he had permanently forced Early from the valley and returned north, burning the valley's crops, mills, and barns in his path. Despite his army's debilitative condition, Early realized he must continue to fight for the valley. He was soon following Sheridan north. On October 9, Early's cavalry engaged the Federals at Tom's Brook. They were defeated, but Early followed undeterred with his infantry. Unaware of Early's advance, Sheridan went into camp around the Belle Grove mansion, northwest of this spot.

On the night of October 18, Early assembled his army along Cedar Creek for an attack. His movements were hidden by the dense woods on the foothills of Massanutten Mountain. At 5 a.m. the surprise attack was launched from positions to the right and left of this bridge. Early and General Kershaw watched the initial advance of the left flank from this spot (Bowman's Mill Ford).

2.1 Right on Long Meadow Road.

The Federals, Thoburn's division, were camped on the hill to your left. They were awakened by the Confederate attack and many were captured before they could even get out of their tents. This road follows Cedar Creek to its confluence with the North Fork of the Shenandoah.

3.8 Road bends sharply to the left.

The right flank of the Confederate attack, Gordon's division, crossed the Shenandoah at this point (Bowman's Ford). They surprised Federal cavalry pickets stationed in the river and swept out of the woods. Once across the river, they marched north, paralleling this road.

4.6 Stop. Left on Water Plant Road (Route 840).

Gordon's division continued north (straight) a few hundred yards at this intersection. In the fields of the Cooley farm, they faced west and charged through a dense morning fog at the stunned Federals. This road is in the center of the Federal retreat and Confederate advance.

5.7 Stop. Right on Route 11 (the Valley Turnpike during the war). Use caution. Moderate traffic.

Near this intersection, the two separate Confederate wings converged on the Federal XIX Corps camp, which was located just across the Valley Turnpike. After a brutal fight, they too were swept up by the Confederate onslaught. They retreated north toward the Federal VI Corps camp, near Belle Grove.

6.3 Left on Route 727. Sign for Cedar Creek Battlefield and Belle Grove.

6.7 Cedar Creek Visitor Center and Belle Grove.

The Visitor Center is open May through December, Monday–Saturday: 10–4, Sunday: 1–5. There is a book shop and exhibit room. Belle Grove is open mid-March through mid-November from 10–4; Sundays: 1–5. Admission charged). The construction of Belle Grove was completed in 1797. Restored and maintained by the National Trust for Historic Preservation of Virginia, Belle Grove is one of the finest architectural sites in the Shenandoah Valley.

Belle Grove, General Sheridan's Headquarters, became the focal point of the Confederate advance. However, Sheridan was not in the house the morning of the attack. He had spent the night in Winchester, after returning from a meeting in Washington. He heard the sounds of artillery and rode toward Cedar Creek at 8 a.m. He reached his demoralized, retreating army around noon and started to reform them north of Middletown. His presence and animation rallied his troops.

In the meantime, the Confederate advance had become disorganized north of Belle Grove. Soldiers had stopped to loot the abandoned Federal camps and their ranks had become intermingled and confused. Confederate officers failed to press their advantage and Early seemed satisfied with the morning victory. The Confederates concentrated their effort on removing captured men, artillery and supplies to the rear.

At 4 p.m. Sheridan counterattacked along a two mile front which was centered on the Valley Turnpike. The Confederates briefly countered, but the onslaught proved too much. For the first and only time in the Civil War, a major battlefield saw the two armies exchange victories in one day. Early's army retreated south of Strasburg and the Valley Campaign was ended.

7.0 Stop. Right on Meadows Mill Road (Route 624).

7.8 Left on Route 625. Dirt Road.

8.7 Stop. Left on Route 627.

Elements of the Union VI Corps held this hill for a few hours against the Confederate attack, before withdrawing north.

12.8 Left on Route 622.

15.7 Left on Route 629.
Use caution crossing railroad tracks at 16.9 Miles.

18.0 Stop. Right on Route 11. Use caution at Route 81 interchange.

19.2 Hupp's Hill Battlefield Park and Study Center on the right.
This hill was used by Confederate artillery, as part of their Cedar Creek assault and withdrawal. It was later occupied by the Union.

20.2 Traffic light. Right on King Street.

20.4 Holliday Street intersection.

End of tour.

Directions: Ride B

0.0 Start at intersection of King Street (Route 55) and Holliday Street. Go east on King Street.

0.2 Traffic light. Straight through intersection with Route 11. Use caution, moderate traffic.
The northern peak of the Massanutten was used as an observation post and signal station by both armies.

5.6 Right on Route 678.
Store on corner in Waterlick. This road parallels Passage Creek through the George Washington National Forest. This isolated area is called Fort Valley .

25.4 Stop. Right on Route 675.
There is a store at this intersection in Kings Crossing. This is a good place to take a break before starting the difficult climb over Edinburg Gap. At 26.6 Miles on the right is a spring. Fill your water bottle and continue the climb. At 27.3 Miles is the top of the gap; use extreme caution on descent. Road is twisting with unprotected drop-offs on your right.

31.1 Stop. Left on Route 11.

31.7 Right on Route 675.
Use caution passing Route 81 intersection.

37.1 Stop. Right on Route 42.
There is a store at this intersection.

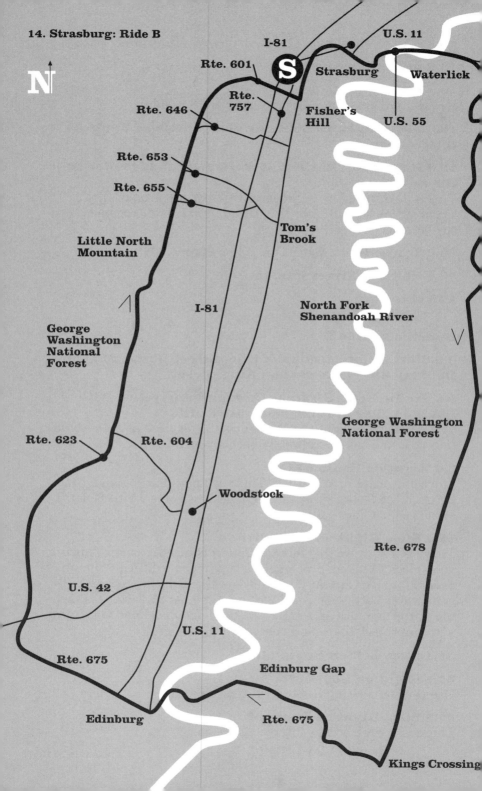

14. Strasburg: Ride B

N

I-81

U.S. 11

Rte. 601

S

Strasburg

Waterlick

Rte. 757

Fisher's Hill

Rte. 646

U.S. 55

Rte. 653

Rte. 655

Tom's Brook

Little North Mountain

North Fork Shenandoah River

I-81

George Washington National Forest

Rte. 623

Rte. 604

George Washington National Forest

Woodstock

Rte. 678

U.S. 42

U.S. 11

Rte. 675

Edinburg Gap

Edinburg

Rte. 675

Kings Crossing

37.2 Left on Route 675.

37.3 Straight on 623, after crossing one lane bridge.
At top of hill bear left at church, still on 623. Little North Mountain and a segment of the George Washington National Forest are on the left. This was known as the Back Road during the war. After Sheridan defeated Early at Third Winchester and Fisher's Hill (see the following description), the Confederates withdrew to Waynesboro. Sheridan controlled the valley, but became nervous about his distance from his supply depots at Martinsburg and Harpers Ferry. Rather than push farther south from Harrisonburg, Sheridan decided to withdraw to Strasburg. He concluded that Early's army was decimated and would no longer pose a threat to the valley. To ensure Union control, Sheridan destroyed much of the valley in his wake.

This operation became known to Shenandoah Valley residents as "the Burning." Sheridan's army formed a line 20 miles across the valley and starting on October 5, 1864 burned most of the farms between Harrisonburg and Strasburg. George Custer commanded the division along this road. Today it is hard to find a barn or mill that predates this period.

The area between Route 655 (47.6 Miles) and Route 633 was the Tom's Brook Battlefield. As Custer's division moved north along Route 623 (Back Road), they were harassed by Confederate cavalry under General Rosser. To the east, Union forces under General Merritt were being pursued by Confederate cavalry under General Lomax. On October 8, Custer and Merritt were ordered to seek out the pursuing Confederates and engage them in battle.

On the morning of October 9 the two forces engaged each other across Tom's Brook (48.6 Miles). The Confederate line stretched across the ridge to the south of the stream, but was not anchored soundly on the left (Little North Mountain). An artillery duel commenced and repeated Federal attempts to break the Confederate line followed. After a few hours Custer ordered a flanking maneuver on the Confederate left. The maneuver was successful and the Confederate cavalry was forced to retreat south in what the Federal cavalry would mockingly call the "Woodstock Races." This was the last large scale cavalry battle of the Civil War.

To view more of the battlefield turn right on Route 655 and then turn left on Route 652 to the end. The association for the Preservation of Civil War Sites has acquired 7.85 acres at this spot. This was the center of the Confederate line. In the future there will be an interpretive display at this location. Return to

Route 623 and continue north.

51.5 Right on Route 601.

After his defeat at Third Winchester, Early withdrew south to this location—Fisher's Hill. This ridge, on your right, was considered one of the strongest defensive locations in the entire Shenandoah Valley (it was dubbed the Gibraltar of the Valley) and had been used by Confederate armies throughout the war.

However, as would happen with the Confederates at Tom's Brook, Early failed to successfully defend his left flank. On September 21, 1864 the two armies skirmished between here and Strasburg. Sheridan detected this Confederate weakness and sent most of George Crook's corps to the west to flank the Confederates. Under cover of darkness Crook marched to the North Mountain woods. The next day he massed his forces and was ready for the assault. The assault pushed the Confederates back and when Crook's forces were joined by the VI Corps to the front, a Union victory was assured. The Confederates lost 1500 men and were forced to retreat to Waynesboro.

Access to the Association for the Preservation of Civil War Sites hiking trail is on the right at 52.8 Miles. Park bike at fence and cross footbridge over Tumbling Run to first interpretive marker. Follow mowed path to the rest of the markers.

53.8 Right on Route 757

Cross over Tumbling Run.

53.9 Stop. Left on Route 601.

Fisher's Hill continues to the Shenandoah River, on the right. The Union VI Corps occupied the high ground to the left.

55.1 Stop. Left on Route 11 North. Use caution, moderate traffic.

The bridge over Tumbling Run, located just before you enter Strasburg, was the location of mass confusion as Confederates retreated after the Battle of Cedar Creek. The Union took many prisoners and supplies as the narrow bridge stalled the Confederate retreat.

56.8 Intersection of King Street (Route 11) and Holliday Street.

End of tour.

15 Port Republic

Start:
Port Republic, Rockingham County, Virginia; I-66 West to Route 81 South. Take Exit 245, Route 659 (Port Republic Road) South to Port Republic. Parking is at the Port Republic Elementary School, on the right after crossing the second bridge.

Ride(s):
15.2 or 18.2 Miles; Flat with some rolling hills.

Hike(s):
No hikes are included in this section. There is a short walk at the Coaling Site (Ride A).

Reading:
Stonewall: A Biography of General Thomas J. Jackson , Byron Farwell, (New York: W.W. Norton & Company, 1992)

The Battles of Cross Keys and Port Republic concluded Stonewall Jackson's 1862 Shenandoah Valley Campaign. After Jackson's victory at Winchester on May 25, Lincoln directed two Union forces to converge on the Shenandoah Valley and cut off Jackson's expected avenue of withdrawal. Jackson eluded their first attempt near Strasburg and continued up (south) the valley.

> *General, he who does not see the hand of God in this is blind, sir, blind.*
>
> General Stonewall Jackson to General Richard Ewell, Port Republic, June 9, 1862

Despite continual harassment and a driving rainstorm, Jackson's outnumbered army kept ahead of the Federals. Jackson decided that he would turn and face the two Federal columns near Port Republic, before they could join their forces. Jackson chose Port Republic as his base of operations because it was located between the North and South rivers, which converge north of town to form the South Fork of the Shenandoah River. A few more miles north of town is the southern end of Massanutten Mountain and the end of the Luray Valley. Port Republic contained an important bridge and two fords that provided the only

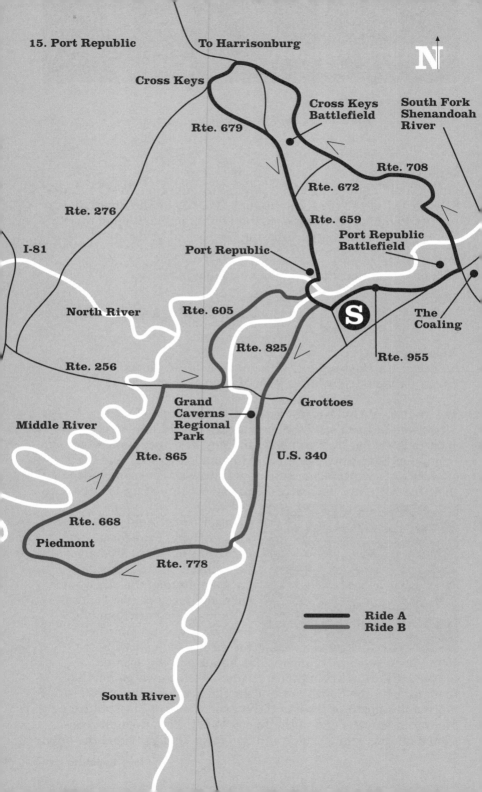

15. Port Republic

To Harrisonburg

Cross Keys

Cross Keys
Battlefield

South Fork
Shenandoah
River

Rte. 679

Rte. 708

Rte. 672

Rte. 659

Rte. 276

Port Republic
Battlefield

I-81

Port Republic

North River

Rte. 605

The
Coaling

Rte. 825

Rte. 955

Rte. 256

Grottoes

Middle River

Grand
Caverns
Regional
Park

Rte. 865

U.S. 340

Rte. 668

Piedmont

Rte. 778

South River

N

S

Ride A
Ride B

crossing of the Shenandoah River and its tributaries for many miles.

One Federal column, under General James Shields, was marching south down the Luray Valley. Another, under John C. Fremont, was following in the Shenandoah Valley. Jackson reached the small town on June 6 and deployed his artillery and most of his troops on a hill west of town to control the crossings. Jackson and his wagon train were almost captured when a lead element of Union cavalry surprised the Confederates and swept into Port Republic on June 8 from the east.

However, Jackson regained control and boldly planned to divide his army and engage each Union army separately. He countered Fremont's pursuit with General Richard Ewell's troops at Cross Keys, a few miles northwest of town. Ewell defeated the inept Fremont at Cross Keys and Jackson was then able to defeat Shields's lead elements north of Port Republic on June 9. Although Jackson's leadership was flawed and he was unable to complete his plan and completely destroy Fremont's force, he once again defeated Union forces by using rapid troop movements and a superior knowledge of the valley's terrain.

The first ride connects the town of Port Republic with the Port Republic and Cross Keys battlefields. Both battlefields are well-preserved, but are mostly private property. The second ride goes through the Piedmont Battlefield (June 5, 1864). This battlefield is also well-preserved. This second ride goes through Grottoes, where you can visit Grand Caverns Regional Park. The two rides have the same starting point and can be easily combined into a 33-mile ride. Although both rides are surrounded by the mountains, there is only moderate climbing involved in this beautiful valley.

Directions: Ride A

0.0 Exit parking at Elementary School to left (west) on Route 659 (Port Republic Road).
The historic section of Port Republic is located to the west, in between the North and South rivers.

0.1 Right on Route 955 (unmarked, first right after school, becomes dirt road).
Before dawn on June 9, 1862 Jackson ordered a brigade, under Charles Winder, to march east and engage the Union force marching south from Conrad's Store (Elkton). Winder's brigade left their camp on the west bank of the North River, crossed the bridge located there, marched through Port Republic and crossed a makeshift bridge over the South River. This makeshift bridge, constructed of planks laid on top of supply wagons, was

located just north of the boat landing on the left. The Confederates then marched north, paralleling this road.

Because of the poor construction of the makeshift bridge, other Confederate troops were slow in supporting Winder's initial advance. Eventually Richard Taylor's brigade crossed and Jackson directed most of his force north in a line across the fields to your left, with the far left anchored on the South Fork of the Shenandoah River.

He was facing 3,000 men, Shields's vanguard under General Erastus Tyler. Tyler had concealed six guns on a coaling (a clearing created by charcoal production), halfway up a low ridge, two miles northeast of Port Republic. If Jackson was to win the battle, he would have to dislodge Tyler's artillery. Jackson sent two regiments of infantry and an artillery battery to the right to flank the artillery. This force split from the other Confederates just north of the current intersection of Route 955 and the railroad crossing.

The Confederate attack on Tyler's artillery was stalled by the thick wilderness. The soldiers had to hack their way through thick mountain laurel and bramble. The Confederate battery made little progress before being forced to turn back and the attack would have to be made by infantry alone. This rough terrain has changed little since the time of the battle.

1.9 Stop. Left on Route 340.
The main battle raged to the left of present-day Route 340. The Union bombardment from the Coaling was devastating on the Confederates, who had little cover on these open fields.

2.5 Right on Route 708.
The Coaling was located on the hill to the left (opposite the Episcopal church). 8.55 acres of the Coaling are currently owned by the Association for the Preservation of Civil War Sites. The Confederates, led by Richard Taylor, eventually fought their way through the woods to the right and attacked the Union artillery emplacement. The Confederates discovered that the artillery was defended by Union infantry and desperate hand-to-hand fighting ensued. Union General Tyler ordered three regiments to charge the Confederates on the hill and Confederate General Taylor wrote later, "There seemed nothing left but to set our backs to the mountain and die hard."

However, just at that time Confederate General Richard Ewell, arriving from Cross Keys, struck the Union left with reinforcements. Tyler was forced to fall back and the Coaling and the captured Union artillery fell into Confederate hands. They turned the guns on the Union and combined with a renewed assault by the Confederates on the Union front. The entire

Union line was forced to retreat. The Battle of Port Republic came to an end with Jackson's valley army suffering over 800 casualties, the greatest of the campaign. Tyler's Union force suffered over 1,000 killed, wounded and captured.

2.5 Stop. Return to Route 340 and continue straight across on Route 708 (west).
The Union infantry were positioned parallel to this road, facing south (left). The Confederates attacked north across these fields. At 3.3 Miles is the bridge over the South Fork of the Shenandoah River. No bridge existed at the time of the battle.

4.1 Stop. Right on Route 708-655.

4.3 Left on Route 708.

6.4 Stop. Straight across Route 672, still on Route 708.
At 7.0 Miles keep to right up short steep hill. You are entering the Cross Keys Battlefield. General Richard Ewell deployed his 6,000 men along this ridge, facing north (straight). His front was about a mile long with his right, a brigade under General Isaac Trimble, anchored along Route 708.

The Federals (10,000 men), under Fremont, marched southeast from Harrisonburg. The battle started in the morning with skirmishing near Cross Keys. After this subsided, an artillery duel commenced and Fremont ordered an infantry attack on Trimble's position. Despite his numerical superiority, Fremont's attack was piecemeal. The Federal attack came across the fields to your left, as you continue north on Route 708. Trimble's brigade remained concealed behind a fence and in woods until the Federals came within range. They then unleashed a devastating volley. The Federals fell back toward the Keezletown Road (Route 276).

8.9 Stop. Right on Route 659 (Port Republic Road).

9.2 Traffic light. Left on Route 276.
The Federal position before and after the battle was along this road.

9.9 Left on Route 679.
This is the village of Cross Keys. The initial skirmishing took place near this intersection. With the Federal attack on the Confederate right unsuccessful, Fremont ordered an attack on the center and left. This advance took place along this road and in the fields and woods to the right. Ewell had massed his artillery in the center of his line and with the arrival of Confederate reinforcements, this Union advance also failed. The Federals fell back to Cross Keys and the battle concluded with

684 Federal casualties to only 288 for the victorious Confederates.

11.2 Stop. Right on Route 659 (Port Republic Road).
The center of the Confederate line, where Ewell massed his artillery was just to the right of this intersection.

14.7 Cross the North River Bridge.
When Jackson decided he needed reinforcements to defeat the Union force north of Port Republic, he ordered the Confederates to withdraw from their position in front of Fremont at Cross Keys. They marched across the river just north of this point and burned the wooden bridge that existed at that time (the abutments are still visible), to prevent Fremont from following.

On the left is a small store and battle map of the area campaign. Also on the left is the Frank Kemper House, where Turner Ashby's body was brought after he was killed near Harrisonburg. The museum is open Sunday 1:30 to 4:00 p.m. Jackson's headquarters at the George Kemper house was located .4 Mile south of this spot. There are many historic buildings along Route 605.

15.0 Cross the South River Bridge.
There was no bridge at this spot during the war.

15.2 Elementary School on the right.

End of tour.

The final and decisive Union charge at the Battle of Piedmont took place up the ridge in front of this battlefield marker.

Directions: Ride B

0.0 Exit Elementary School to the left on Route 659.

0.1 Left on Route 825 (sign for Grottoes).
At 2.0 Miles there is a restaurant on the right as you enter Grottoes.

2.5 Stop. Straight across Route 256, still on Route 825 (Dogwood Avenue).
At 2.8 Miles is Grand Caverns Regional Park. These caves were discovered in 1804. During the Civil War both Confederate and Union troops were housed in the Great Cathedral Hall and Grand Ballroom in the Caverns. The park is open daily 9–5 from March through October. Admission is charged.

5.6 Stop. Right on Route 778. Cross the South River Bridge.

7.0 Stop. Straight across Route 865, still on Route 778.

9.5 Stop. Right on Route 668 (Battlefield Road).
This small crossroads is Piedmont. The Battle of Piedmont took place on June 5, 1864. After his humiliating defeat at New Market on May 15, Union General Franz Sigel was replaced by General David Hunter. Hunter, like his predecessors, marched south to attempt to drive the Confederates from the valley. His 8,500 troops reached Harrisonburg with little resistance. At Harrisonburg Hunter learned the Confederates were forming a defensive line at Mount Crawford, so he decided to march to Port Republic and continue southeast to threaten the rail line near Waynesboro. This would cut off Staunton and force the Confederates to fight Hunter away from their strong defensive position at Mount Crawford.

The Confederates, about 5,000 men, were also under new leadership. General William Jones was the newly appointed head of the Department of Southwestern Virginia. Although criticized for a caustic personality that earned him the sobriquet "Grumble," Jones was a good officer. After belatedly learning of Hunter's move toward Port Republic, he rushed his force to this area. He deployed his infantry in an inverted L shape with the toe anchored on the North River (to the northwest of this inter-section). His reserves were placed south and east of the intersection, with his cavalry support as far south as Round Hill (visible south of this intersection).

The battle started shortly after dawn as a cavalry skirmish at Mt. Meridian, 4.5 miles north of here. The Federals were delayed, but when they received artillery support, the

Confederate cavalry force had to withdraw south to Piedmont.

By mid-morning Federal infantry reached the forward Confederate lines and the main battle was underway. The Federals massed 22 artillery pieces on the heights to the front of this spot, near the road, and fired on the angle in the Confederate line. Federal infantry were massed to the west of the road. Fighting raged all day with no real advantage, despite the fact that the Confederate artillery was silenced after a few hours.

However, Hunter noticed a gap in the Confederate line and ordered Thoburn's regiment to cross the road to the southeast and attack up the ridge (to the right) at this weakness. Hand-to-hand fighting ensued and Jones led a small reserve force to stop the attack. Jones was killed by a bullet to the head and fell from his horse. His death combined with pressure on all sides broke the Confederate ranks and they fled. Inexplicably, Confederate cavalry under John Vaughan, failed to support the infantry and a rout was ensured. Confederates lost over 600 casualties and had over 1,000 men taken prisoner. For the first time in the war, the Union controlled the entire Shenandoah Valley.

12.9 Stop. Left on Rockfish Road (Route 865).

13.9 Stop. Right on Route 256 (Weyer's Cave Road).

14.3 Left on Route 605 (Lee Roy Road).
There are many historic buildings along Route 605 as you enter Port Republic. The town has been placed on the Virginia Historic Register.

17.6 Stop. Right on Route 659.
There is a store and historic marker at this intersection.

18.1 Elementary School on right.

End of tour.

16 Middleburg

Start:
Middleburg, Loudoun County, Virginia; I-495 (Capital Beltway)
to I-66 West. Take Exit 57, Route 50 West. Turn left at
Pendleton Street in downtown Middleburg. Parking is one block
on the left.

Ride(s):
33.2 Miles; Rolling hills with a few steep climbs. This ride contains five miles of dirt roads.

Hike(s):
Sky Meadows State Park is located 12 miles west of Middleburg.
Turn left on Route 17 and follow sign to entrance. The area of
the park was the site of several Confederate encampments and
the Mosby Rangers hid in these mountains. Mt. Bleak was the
home of Dr. Thomas Settle, who pronounced John Brown dead
after his hanging. There are many hiking trails here and the
Appalachian Trail runs through the park.

Reading:
Ranger Mosby, Virgil Carrington Jones, (EPM Publications, Inc.,
McLean, VA, 1972)

On the evening of March 8, 1863 John S. Mosby led 29 of his
rangers towards Fairfax Courthouse. By the time the sun rose
the next morning, Mosby had indeed "mounted the stars." While
his original intention had been to Capture Sir Percy Wyndham,
an Englishman in the employ of
the Union cavalry, Mosby and
his men came away with a big-
ger prize—Brigadier General
Edwin Stoughton. Stoughton,
the youngest general in the
Union army, was caught sleep-
ing off the effects of a champagne party. In addition to
Stoughton, Mosby left Fairfax with two captains, thirty enlisted
men, and fifty-eight horses. Upon hearing of the raid Lincoln
wryly noted, "Well I'm sorry for that. I can make new brigadier
generals, but I can't make horses."

> *I shall mount the stars tonight*
> *or sink lower than the*
> *plummet ever sounded.*
>
> John S. Mosby, March 8, 1863

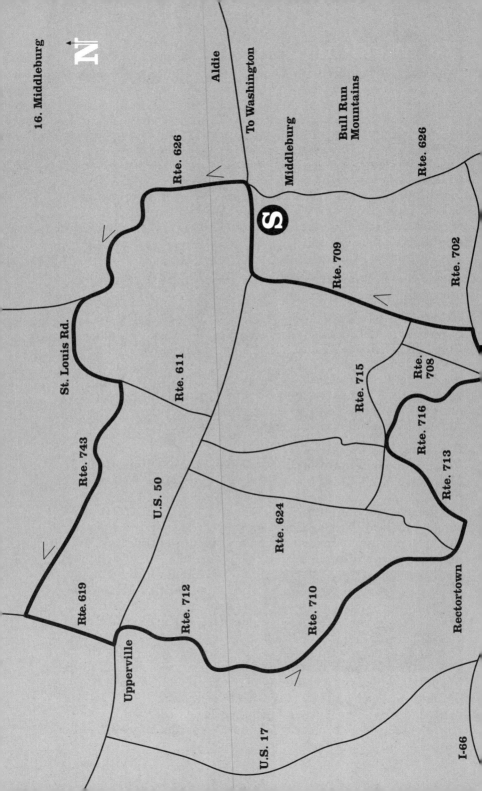

16. Middleburg

N

Aldie

To Washington

Bull Run Mountains

Middleburg

S

Rte. 626

Rte. 626

Rte. 709

Rte. 702

St. Louis Rd.

Rte. 611

Rte. 743

Rte. 715

Rte. 708

Rte. 716

U.S. 50

Rte. 713

Rte. 624

Rte. 619

Rte. 712

Rte. 710

Rectortown

Upperville

U.S. 17

I-66

This raid made Mosby famous throughout both the North and South. Before the war was over his name would be heard many more times and today historians consider him the foremost guerrilla leader of the Civil War. Mosby's understanding of partisan warfare enabled his small command (never more than 800 men) to control a large area of northern Virginia, despite the efforts of large Union forces directed against him. Because of his success Loudoun and Fauquier counties became known as Mosby's Confederacy.

This ride goes through the heart of Mosby's Confederacy past many of the sites associated with his command. In addition, from June 17–21, 1863 a series of cavalry battles took place along the turnpike (now Route 50) between Aldie and Upperville. This important engagement is often overlooked because it took place between Brandy Station and Gettysburg. While the Confederates, under Jeb Stuart, were driven back by the Federals commanded by Alfred Pleasanton, the Confederates prevented the Federals from discovering the whereabouts of the Confederate infantry, who were moving north in the Shenandoah Valley. The five days of fighting caused over a thousand casualties.

This unique barn is located in the heart of Virginia horse country.

This area of historic towns, large horse farms and beautiful countryside remains largely unchanged since the time of the Civil War. While riding your bike along these small country roads it is easy to imagine Mosby's rangers galloping towards another skirmish or secret rendezvous.

Directions:

0.0 Exit parking lot to right on Pendleton Street.

0.1 Stop. Right on Main Street, (Route 50).
The town of Middleburg and the surrounding countryside was the location of heavy fighting on June 17–19, 1863. Confederate cavalry were camped from Middleburg to Aldie when the Union attacked on the afternoon of June 17. One Union brigade under Judson Kilpatrick attacked the Confederates near Aldie while Colonel Alfred Duffie's 1st Rhode Island attacked Stuart at Middleburg. Both Union forces were decimated by the Confederates in this badly planned affair. Colonel Duffie's command did not reach his own lines until the next morning and by that time he had lost 214 of his 300 men. Stuart withdrew all the Confederates to a ridge west of town on June 18.

0.2 Left on Route 626 (traffic light at intersection).
The Red Fox Inn is located on this corner. Mosby met with Stuart on the afternoon of June 17 at this Inn.

0.2 Bear right on Route 626 at split.

2.6 Bear right at intersection just after crossing Goose Creek, still on Route 626.

4.0 Stop. Straight at intersection of Pot House Road and Foxcroft Road. Still on Route 626 (Pot House Road).

5.0 Left on Saint Louis Road.

7.2 Right on Webourne Road (Route 743).
This is a hard-packed dirt road. Look for the unique barn to your left.

9.5 Stop. Right on Millville Road (still Route 743).
Road is paved at this point.

10.7 Stop. Intersection with Greengarden Road. Continue straight, still on Route 743.
This becomes a dirt road again. On October 14, 1864 Mosby's men captured $173,000 from a Union train near Harpers Ferry. The next day they divided the money north of this intersection. Mosby refused his share, so his men bought him a thoroughbred named "Croquette."

12.0 Stop. Road ends, turn left on Trappe Road (Route 619).

14.3 Stop. Left on Route 50 (John S. Mosby Highway).
Entering Upperville. Forced back by superior numbers after the fighting around Middleburg on June 17-19, Stuart rode toward Ashby Gap, where he could form a strong defensive position in the mountains and where he could be reinforced by Confederate infantry. To protect his withdrawal he turned and struck the pursuing Federals at Upperville. The Confederates checked the Federal advance east and north of town and safely reached Ashby's Gap at 6 p.m. The Federals went into camp that night and the engagement came to an end.

14.5 Right on Route 712.
Before making this turn you may want to continue on Route 50 for a short distance into Upperville. Less than a mile ahead is a small store (the only store before returning to Middleburg). About .3 mile further on the left is a small stone house (unmarked). Heroes Von Borcke, a German who served on Jeb Stuart's staff, was brought here after being seriously wounded between Middleburg and Upperville. Von Borcke describes his hazardous ambulance ride from the battlefield to the house:

> *Meanwhile, the Federals were rapidly advancing, and numbers of their shells burst so near the ambulance that the driver was seized with fright, and believing that anyhow I was nearly dead drove off at a gallop over the rocky road regardless of my agonized groans, every movement of the vehicle causing a fresh effusion of blood from my wound. At last I could stand it no longer and crawling up to him, I put my cocked pistol to his head and made him understand that I should blow out his brains if he continued his cowardly flight.*

Von Borcke was unable to return to duty after his wounding, but always remained loyal to the Confederacy. On his return to Germany he flew the Confederate flag from the rampart of his ancestral castle. Return on Route 50 to turn on Route 712.

17.1 Left on Rectortown Road (Route 710).
Prepare to shift gears often along this winding, hilly road.

20.9 Straight at intersection of Route 710 and Route 624.
This is Rectortown. This small crossroads was considered to be the capital of Mosby's Confederacy. In September 1864 some of

Mosby's men were accused of killing Lieutenant Charles McMaster, while he tried to surrender. In turn the Union executed six of Mosby's Rangers in Front Royal, Virginia.

In retaliation Mosby received permission to execute Union prisoners. On November 6, 1864 twenty Union prisoners were ordered to line up in Rectortown and draw lots. Those drawing a number were pulled out of line to be led to their execution. One of those drawing a slip was a young drummer boy, who was spared. His substitute and the other six men were led to a spot near Berryville where they were to be hung or shot. Two men escaped and two survived but Mosby got across his message. There were no more executions of Mosby's men.

A short distance west of here on Route 624 was the Rectortown railroad station. Union General George McClellan had his headquarters here when he received word on November 7, 1862 that he was being relieved of the command of the Army of the Potomac.

21.3 Left on Route 713.
The brick building on the right was a store during the war. Mosby and his men often met here.

23.4 Right on Route 716 (dirt road).
This intersection of five country roads was the site of a skirmish on January 1, 1864. A company of Union cavalry started from Harpers Ferry in search of Mosby. They were ambushed at this spot and suffered 57 casualties. Mosby had struck again.

Lakeland (private residence) is located 1.8 miles further north on Route 713. On December 21, 1864 Mosby was critically wounded while visiting this house. Union cavalry surprised him and a Corporal Kane of the 13th New York Cavalry shot him through the rear window of the house. Before they could enter Mosby hid his uniform coat and convinced the Union soldiers that he was a Lieutenant Johnson of the 6th Virginia Cavalry. Thinking he was mortally wounded anyway, the Union soldiers left him. He was carried to a nearby house, where he recovered from this wound—his seventh of the war. If you have ridden north on Route 713 to Lake-land, turn around and return to the intersection with Route 716.

25.8 Stop. Right on Route 708 (road unmarked).

25.8 Stop. Left on Route 702.

27.0 Stop. Left on Route 709.
At 27.9 Miles is the intersection with Route 708. 0.5 mile to the left is the Hathaway House. During the spring of 1863, Mosby arranged to have his wife stay here so he could visit her on occa-

sion while conducting raids in the area. During one of his visits the Union learned of his whereabouts and surrounded the house. Mosby barely escaped by climbing onto a tree and hanging on a branch while they searched the house and a Union officer interrogated his wife.

31.8 Stop. Right on Route 50 (John S. Mosby Highway). Use caution. Moderate traffic on this road. This ridge was used by Stuart's artillery to bombard the advancing Federals on June 19, 1863.

33.1 Right on Pendleton Street, downtown Middleburg.

33.2 Left into parking.

End of tour.

17 Culpeper

Start:
Culpeper, Culpeper County, Virginia; I-95 to Exit 130, Route 3
West. After crossing the James Madison Highway and entering
Culpeper turn right on Main Street. Right on East Davis Street
to parking at corner of Commerce Street and East Davis Street,
across from Amtrak Station.

Ride(s):
42.5 ; Rolling hills.

Hike(s):
Walking tour of Culpeper, detailed map of historic buildings
available from Culpeper Chamber of Commerce at 133 West
Davis Street.

Reading:
Clash of Cavalry: The Battle of Brandy Station, Fairfax Downey,
(David McKay Company, New York, 1959)

The Culpeper area was the location of some of the Civil War's
largest encampments and important battles. After the
Confederate victories at Fredericksburg and Chancellorsville,
Robert E. Lee concentrated his army around Culpeper. From
here he would launch the inva-
sion of the North that would
result in Gettysburg less than
one month later. On June 8,
1863 J.E.B. Stuart held a grand
review of his cavalry for General
Lee in a field at Brandy Station,
northeast of Culpeper. The assembled cavalry, more than ten
thousand men, stretched for a mile as they paraded in front of
Lee's staff. Regimental bands played and artillery fired blank
charges as they engaged in a mock battle.

> The Battle of Brandy Station made the Federal Cavalry.
>
> Confederate Major Henry McClellan

Unbeknownst to the Confederates, the Federal cavalry could
hear this pageantry from their positions just across the
Rappahannock River. On the morning of June 9 a Union force of
cavalry and infantry, under Major General Alfred Pleasonton,

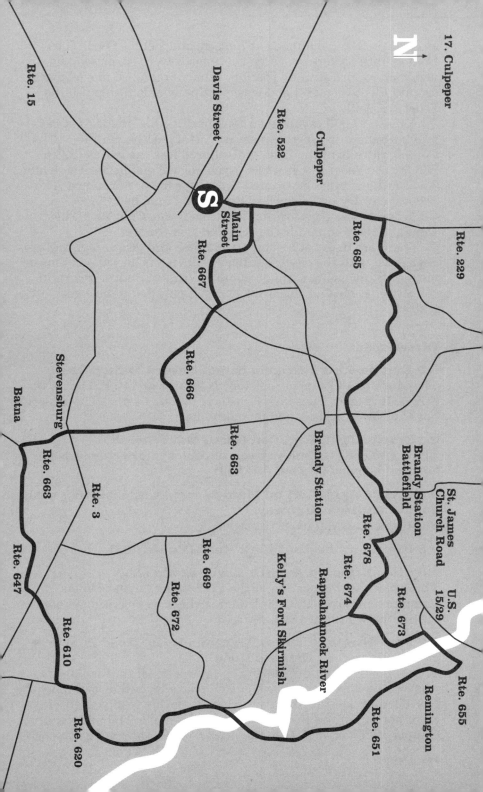

17. Culpeper

N

Culpeper

Davis Street

Rte. 522

Main Street

Rte. 685

Rte. 229

Rte. 15

Rte. 667

Rte. 666

Stevensburg

Rte. 663

Batna

Rte. 663

Rte. 3

Brandy Station

Brandy Station Battlefield

St. James Church Road

U.S. 15/29

Rte. 678

Rte. 674

Rte. 673

Remington

Rte. 655

Rappahannock River

Kelly's Ford Skirmish

Rte. 669

Rte. 672

Rte. 647

Rte. 610

Rte. 651

Rte. 620

S

crossed the Rappahannock at Beverly and Kelly's Ford. The Confederate pickets guarding these fords were surprised and driven back toward Brandy Station. Stuart organized his defenses around Fleetwood Hill and was eventually able to repulse the Federal assault.

Almost 19,000 cavalrymen took part in this, the largest cavalry engagement in North American history. Although the Confederates held the field and suffered less casualties (523 to 866 for the Federals), it was a psychological victory for the Union. The southern press excoriated Stuart for his performance. The Federal cavalry had surprised Stuart and matched the Confederate troopers for the first time in the Civil War. They would be their equal for the remainder of the war.

There are many other important sites and geographic features associated with the Civil War near Culpeper. This rides connects most of these, going through some of Virginia's most beautiful countryside. Most of the roads are well paved and have very little traffic.

Directions:

0.0 Exit parking on Davis Street toward Main Street.
The Museum of Culpeper History is located at 140 E. Davis Street. It is open Tuesday–Saturday; 11 a.m.–4 p.m. The museum has Civil War displays and memorabilia.

0.1 Traffic light. Right on North Main Street.
The house on the northwest corner of this intersection was the boyhood home of General A.P. Hill.

0.5 Traffic light. Left on Main Street at intersection with James Madison Highway.
Start up hill as you leave Culpeper.

2.8 Right on Chestnut Fork Road (Route 685).

4.0 Stop. Right on Auburn Road (Route 685).
This area was the location of the Civil War's largest Union encampment. Over 100,000 Union soldiers were stationed here during the winter of 1863–1864.

8.2 Stop. Straight across Alanthus Road. Road is now called Fleetwood Heights Road.
This is Brandy Station. During the war a small railroad depot was located here on the Orange and Alexandria Railroad (now the Norfolk and Southern). As you ride along this road you enter the main portion of the Brandy Station Battlefield. The hill you are climbing is Fleetwood Hill, the main Confederate defensive posi-

tion. From here Stuart was able to stall the Federal advance from the south (your right) with a single gun.

10.0 Beverly Ford Road on left.
Turn here for a brief tour of the northern portion of the Brandy Station Battlefield (see map). The Confederates were able to turn back the Union advance from Beverly's Ford from their position near St. James Church.

10.5 Stop. Straight across James Madison Highway (Route 15-29). Use caution.

10.6 Left on Elkwood Road (Route 678), first road over railroad tracks.

10.8 Right on Kellysville Road (Route 674).

12.8 Left on Newbys Shop Road (Route 673).

14.6 Stop. Right on Remington Road (Business 15-29).
Use caution crossing bridge over the Rappahannock River into Remington. Remington was called Rappahannock Station during the Civil War. In October 1863 the Confederates forced the Union out of the Culpeper area and established entrenchments on the east bank of the Rappahannock. The center of the line was Rappahannock Station and its important railroad bridge.

On November 7 the Union VI Corps surprised the Confederates with an unusual night attack. The battle raged back and forth over the earthworks, but eventually the Confederates were overwhelmed. Many Confederates were forced to swim across the river to escape capture. They lost 1300 men and a number of supplies to the victorious Federals. It was one of only a handful of successful night attacks by either side during the Civil War.

15.4 Right on Main Street (Route 655).

15.6 Right on Route 651 (first right after crossing railroad

tracks).

20.0 Right on Edwards Shop Road (Route 620).
Use caution crossing uneven bridge over Rappahannock River.

Kelly's Ford was an important Civil War crossing because the river was very shallow and narrow at this point. On March 17, 1863 3,000 Union cavalrymen, under Brigadier General William Averell, crossed here to probe Confederate defenses in the area. They immediately came under fire by Confederate pickets on the west bank. In addition, the Confederates had blocked the road with an abatis. After a short fight the Federals cleared the abatis, scattered the small Confederate force and headed north toward Brandy Station.

About a mile north of the ford they encountered about 800 Confederate cavalrymen under General Fitzhugh Lee. Lee was a former West Point rival of Averell and had been taunting his classmate during the previous months. At one point Lee had sent a message to Averell telling him to come across the river and bring some coffee with him. Lee now had his wish and a fierce cavalry battle ensued.

A series of charges and countercharges took place along a stone wall. The outmanned Confederates paid the higher price in casualties. They lost 133 men, compared with the Federals 78. One of the Confederate casualties was Major John Pelham, one of the South's most promising young officers. The Federals withdrew when they discovered J.E.B. Stuart was at the scene (he had been overseeing a court-martial in Culpeper). Before leaving, Averell left a sack of coffee with a note attached: "Dear Fitz. Here's your coffee. Here's your visit. How do you like it?"

The Union cavalry, under Alfred Duffie and Maxcy Gregg crossed here again on the morning of June 9 as part of the Battle of Brandy Station. They headed four miles west, before dividing their columns. Gregg's force rode north and joined the main Federal assault around Fleetwood Hill, while Duffie continued west to threaten the Confederate rear near Stevensburg.

20.4 Left on Edwards Shop Road (immediately after crossing bridge).

20.6 Left at Stones Mill Road intersection, still on Edwards Shop Road (Route 620).

25.8 Stop. Right on Elys Ford Road (Route 610).
This road leads to Elys Ford, an important Rapidan River crossing point. The Union used this crossing on their way to Chancellorsville (XII Corps) and The Wilderness (II Corps).

26.3 Left on Route 647 (Revercomb Road).

27.2 Stop. Right on Route 3 (Germana Highway).
This road leads to Germana Ford, another important Rapidan River crossing used by both armies. Colonel Alfred Duffie's cavalry regiment was sent west from Kelly's Ford to Stevensburg to harass the Confederate rear as part of the Brandy Station attack. After being repelled by the 2nd South Carolina two miles west of this spot, Duffie's command was ordered to turn north to join the assault at Brandy Station. He arrived too late to affect the outcome.

27.3 Left on Route 647 (Batna Road).

31.2 Stop. Right on Route 663 (Rogues Road).
Dozens of small skirmishes were fought in this area as the Confederate army drove the Union from around Culpeper in August 1862 and October 1863. A few miles southwest of Batna is Raccoon Ford. On August 17, 1862 two Federal cavalry regiments, under Colonel Thornton Brodhead, crossed the Rapidan River at that spot. They were given orders to investigate a possible Confederate advance on the Union force near Culpeper.

Brodhead's command was allowed to roam behind Confederate lines unmolested. They headed south and had two important encounters. First, they captured Major Norman Fitzhugh and a satchel containing orders from Robert E. Lee to J.E.B. Stuart. These orders detailed Lee's plan to attack the Union army while it was spread out around Culpeper. Their next encounter was with Stuart and his command. They surprised them at their headquarters at Verdiersville and Stuart and other officers barely escaped. The Federals embarassed Stuart by taking his beloved plumed hat, which he lost in his flight.

34.2 Stop. Straight across Route 3, still on Route 663 (now called Stevensburg Road).
A store is located just to the right on Route 3.

35.9 Left on Route 666 (Braggs Corner Road).

39.0 Stop. Straight across Route 15-29. Use caution.

39.1 Left on Route 667 (Nalles Mill Road).

41.1 Stop. Left on Business Route 29 (James Madison Highway). Use caution, moderate traffic.

41.9 Traffic light. Left on Main Street at split.

42.4 Traffic light. Left on Davis Street.

42.5 Parking on left.

End of tour.

18 Fredericksburg

Start:
Fredericksburg, Spotsylvania County, Virginia; Interstate 95 to
Exit 130 (East on Route 3 to Downtown Fredericksburg). Right on
Littlepage Street to end. Right on Business Route 1 (Lafayette
Boulevard) to Fredericksburg Battlefield Visitor Center on right.
Parking in rear.

Ride(s):
10.6 or 12.7 Miles; Flat with one hill on short ride, two hills on
long ride

Hike(s):
Walking tour of Fredericksburg. The full tour is about 4 miles and
includes many Colonial and Civil War history sites. Starts at
Visitor Center at 706 Caroline Street, where a detailed map is
available.

Reading:
The Angel of Marye's Heights, Richard Nunn Lanier, (The
Fredericksburg Press, Fredericksburg, VA, 1961)

There was no Civil War General who knew his limitations better
than Ambrose Burnside. While he sometimes demonstrated compe-
tence as a corps commander, he realized he did not have the exper-
tise or imagination to develop a battle plan for the entire Army of
the Potomac. However, after
repeated pressure from Lincoln,
Burnside reluctantly agreed to
take the command on November 7,
1862. At first his self-deprecation
seemed exaggerated. In a week he
had the previously stagnant army
moving south. By November 18 it
seemed as if he had successfully
flanked the Confederates and stood poised to take Fredericksburg
with little opposition.

> *I probably knew less than any
> other corps commander of the
> position and relative strengths of
> the several corps of the army.*
>
> General Ambrose E. Burnside,
> November 7, 1862

But then a combination of bad luck, bad weather and
Burnside's own ineptness prevented the Federals from crossing the
Rappahannock River and seizing Fredericksburg. The delay

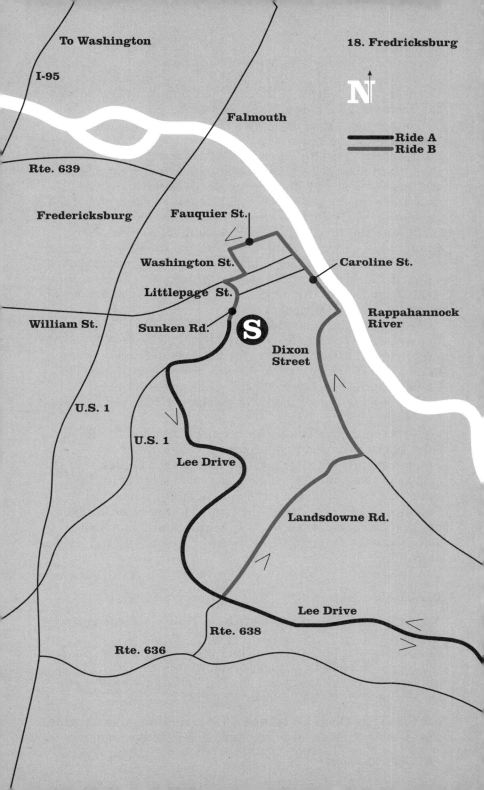

To Washington

18. Fredricksburg

I-95

N

Falmouth

Ride A
Ride B

Rte. 639

Fredericksburg

Fauquier St.

Washington St.

Caroline St.

Littlepage St.

S

Rappahannock
River

William St.

Sunken Rd.

Dixon
Street

U.S. 1

U.S. 1

Lee Drive

Landsdowne Rd.

Lee Drive

Rte. 638

Rte. 636

allowed Lee to be certain of Burnside's movements. By November 30 he had the Army of Northern Virginia in place at Fredericksburg and guarding all the Rappahannock fords. When Burnside was finally able to launch an assault on December 11, the Federals faced a deeply entrenched foe.

For the next three days, with the main battle occuring on December 13, the Federals would attempt to dislodge the Confederates. Despite acts of individual and group heroism, their effort was futile. Under cover of dark and a driving rain-storm, the Federals withdrew across the Rappahannock. The attack cost them over 12,000 casualties. It remains one of the most misguided efforts in American military history.

In May 1863 the Union again assaulted Fredericksburg, when the VI Corps attempted to flank the Confederates as part of the Battle of Chancellorsville. This time they succeeded in capturing Marye's Heights, only to be defeated at Salem Church, west of Fredericksburg. Once again the Federals were forced to retreat across the Rappahannock.

Before starting your ride please visit the battlefield Visitor Center, where you can learn more about the battle and pick up supplemental literature. The ride follows the Confederate posi-tions along the ridge west and south of Fredericksburg. The remains of their trenches are still visible. The National Park Service has erected a number of markers to help you interpret the battle.

If you choose the longer tour, you will descend the small ridge to the river and then proceed through oldtown Fredericksburg. On your return to the Visitor Center, you will climb the same hill that challenged Union soldiers as they attempted to take Marye's Heights. Adjacent to the Visitor Center is the Sunken Road, the Confederates' most formidable position and one of the Civil War's most famous landmarks. If you choose the longer tour, be aware of automobile and pedestri-an traffic.

Directions: Ride A

0.0 Exit center to right. South on Route 1 (Lafayette Boulevard).
Fredericksburg National Cemetery is on your right as you start the tour. Confederate artillery occupied this hill during the Battle of Fredericksburg and the Federal assault on Marye's Heights on May 3, 1863 (Salem Church).

0.4 Straight through Route 3 intersection. Use caution.
The center of the Confederate line was anchored along this

ridge. Although it is only 150 feet above the Rappahannock, it was high enough to give the Confederates a distinct advantage over the advancing Federals. In addition, it was over three miles from Union artillery positions on the heights east of the Rappahannock River. This distance prevented the Union artillery from effectively bombarding these positions.

0.6 Left on Lee Drive. Use caution.
Entering Fredericksburg-Spotsylvania National Military Park. Trenches are located along this road to your left. At 0.8 Miles is the Lee Hill Exhibit Shelter. Major General George Pickett's division occupied this line as it curves to the west.

3.2 Stop. Straight at Landsdowne Road intersection, still on Lee Drive.
At 4.7 Miles is Exhibit 3—the Federal Breakthrough. At this point the Federals, under George Meade, briefly broke the Confederate line. The Federals swept across this road before being driven back by Early's and Taliaferro's divisions.

5.3 Stop. Road ends. Turn around and head back on Lee Drive.
Exhibit 4 (Prospect Hill) is here. The Confederates had fourteen artillery pieces on this hill. A monument to George Meade is located northeast of this spot. Hamilton's crossing is a short distance east of here. D.H. Hill's men protected this important railroad junction.

7.4 Stop. Continue straight on Lee Drive. Ride split.

10.0 Stop. Right on Route 1 (Lafayette Boulevard).

10.6 Left at Visitor Center. Return to parking. Use caution crossing Route 1.

End of tour

Directions: Ride B

Follow directions for Ride A to Mile 7.4; turn right on Landsdowne Road (Route 638).
You are now leaving the Fredericksburg-Spotsylvania National Military Park. The sloping woods and field to your right was the site of intense fighting on December 13. Starting at 1 p.m. John Gibbon's division advanced on the Confederates in coordination with Meade's advance further east. They got past the railroad embankment and into the woods before confusion and intense fire drove them back to the Old Richmond Road (Business 17).

9.1 Stop. Left on Business 17 (Dixon Street).
Use caution on this road. There can be heavy traffic, especially
during weekdays. After crossing the Rappahannock, the Union
assembled artillery to the west of this road and used the road to
move troops south to support Meade's attack.

**10.0 Straight through intersection with Route 3. Use
caution. Now on Route 2.**

**10.4 Right at intersection. Still on Route 2 (Dixon
Street).**

10.5 Stop. Left on Caroline Street.
Entering historic downtown Fredericksburg. To attack the
heights west of town, the Union had to assemble pontoon
bridges, cross the Rappahannock and gain a foothold in
Fredericksburg. To delay this action, the Confederates kept
1,600 troops posted in basements, rifle pits and behind stone
walls in downtown Fredericksburg. They successfully delayed
the Union crossing for most of the day (December 11), despite a
Union bombardment that fired more than 5,000 shells into
Fredericksburg.

The Confederates retreated slowly through the streets, keep-
ing up their fire as the Federals landed in Fredericksburg. When
they reached the safety of their lines on Marye's Heights they
were greeted with cheers for their bravery. Fredericksburg was
left in ruins from the fight and scars are still visible on many
buildings. Please obey all traffic signals as you proceed north on
Caroline Street to the next turn. There are many restaurants
and stores located in this area and it is a good place to take a
break.

11.4 Left on Fauquier Street.
You are now heading in the same direction as the Union assault
on Marye's Heights. Please stop at all cross streets. Many of
these houses existed at the time of the battle. With the impend-
ing battle, the residents were forced to flee. General James
Longstreet wrote the following description:

> *The evacuation of the place by the distressed women and
> helpless men was a painful sight. Many were almost
> destitute and had nowhere to go, but, yielding to the cruel
> necessities of war, they collected their portable effects and
> turned their back on town.*

Most returned to damaged and looted homes. In May 1863,
they would have to flee once more when the Union again
assaulted the city.

11.7 Stop. Right on one way street (unmarked). Kenmore Park and Hugh Mercer Monument are straight ahead.

11.7 Left on first street (unmarked). This street crosses the park.

11.7 Left on Washington Street.
At 11.9 Miles the Confederate Cemetery is located on the right.

12.0 Right on William Street. Yield to traffic.

12.3 Left on Littlepage Street. Traffic light.

12.4 Right on Hanover Street.
The main Union assault on the Confederate entrenchments at the Sunken Road occurred just to the left of this road. (Most houses were not here and the Federals had very little cover during their assault.) The repeated assaults were futile and when they finally stopped the Union had incurred 7,000 casualties compared with only 1,200 for the Confederates. Not a single Union soldier reached the wall. The night of December 13 the dead and wounded laid on this slope unattended. Those soldiers who were not wounded were pinned down by Confederate fire and could not return to entrenchments near the river. The night was bitterly cold and these soldiers were forced to pull their dead comrades on top of them to keep from freezing.

12.5 Left on The Sunken Road.
The Confederates most secure defenses were located here. Part of the original stone wall can be seen to your left. Further down the slope is the Kirkland Monument. The monument was raised in memory of Richard Kirkland, a nineteen-year-old Confederate sergeant, who risked his life to bring water to the suffering Union wounded on the night of December 13. He was called the Angel of Marye's Heights for his compassion.

12.7 Visitor Center on left. Walk bicycle to parking.

End of tour.

19 Chancellorsville-Wilderness

Start:
Chancellorsville Visitor Center, Spotsylvania County, Virginia;
Interstate 95 to Exit 130 (Route 3) West. Chancellorsville Visitor
Center is on the right as you enter the Fredericksburg-
Spotsylvania National Military Park.

Ride(s):
13.7 or 28.9 Miles; Flat with a few small hills. Part of the ride is
on a wide dirt trail. A mountain bike or hybrid is recommended.

Hike(s):
1, 2, or 4 Miles. Detailed maps of the Chancellorsville History
Trail, Gordon Flank Attack Trail, and Hazel Grove-Fairview
Trail are available at the Visitor Center.

Reading:
Into The Wilderness with the Army of the Potomac, Robert Garth
Scott, (Indiana University Press, Bloomington, IN, 1985)
Chancellorsville 1863, Ernest B. Ferguson, (Alfred A. Knopf,
New York,N.Y., 1992)

Chancellorsville and The Wilderness were fought a year apart,
within a few miles of each other . Both were the opening battles
of spring and another attempt by the Union to flank Lee and
advance on Richmond. Both battles had to be conducted in a
dense wooded area that made
maneuvering difficult. However,
there were many differences
between the two battles and a
substantial difference in their
outcome. The year between May
1863 and May 1864 saw many
changes in the two opposing
armies. Thomas "Stonewall"
Jackson was wounded by his own men during Chancellorsville.
He died a week later on May 10, 1863. His death sent the South
into a period of mourning and crippled the Confederate army.
Lee had lost his ablest corps commander and the man responsible for the brilliant flanking march that routed the Union at

> *He has lost his left arm, but I
> have lost my right.*
>
> Robert E. Lee responding to
> news of Stonewall Jackson's
> worsening condition on
> May 7, 1863

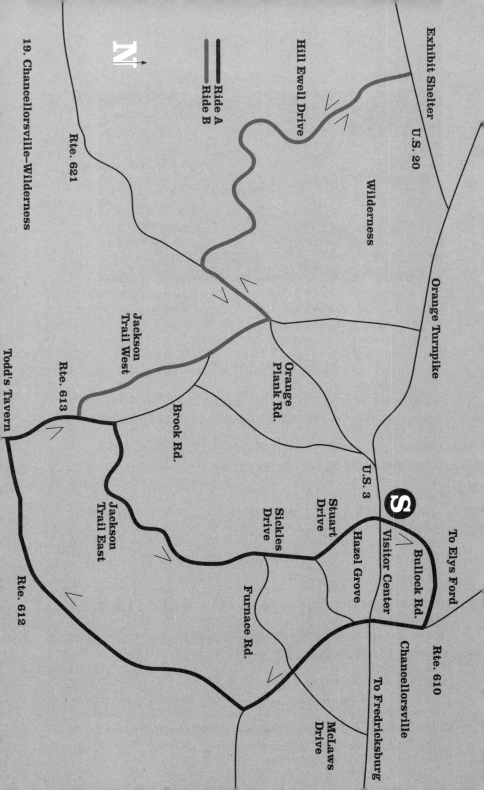

19. Chancellorsville–Wilderness

N

Ride A
Ride B

Exhibit Shelter

U.S. 20

Hill Ewell Drive

Wilderness

Orange Turnpike

Rte. 621

Jackson Trail West

Orange Plank Rd.

Rte. 613

Brock Rd.

U.S. 3

Todd's Tavern

Jackson Trail East

Sickles Drive

Stuart Drive

Hazel Grove

Visitor Center

S

Bullock Rd.

To Elys Ford

Rte. 610

Chancellorsville

To Fredricksburg

Rte. 612

Furnace Rd.

McLaws Drive

Chancellorsville. Lee had also lost many other veterans during this hard year.

While the Union army suffered its share of deprivation during this year, it had a single addition that compensated for many of its losses. On March 3, 1864 Ulysses S. Grant received word that he was to assume command of all Union armies. After visiting Lincoln in Washington, Grant attached himself to the Army of the Potomac, then in its winter camps around Culpeper. Grant would stay with the Army of the Potomac for the rest of the war. Unlike his predecessors, no matter the outcome of any battle, he would never retreat north of the Rappahannock River.

> *The foe that held his guarded hills,*
> *Must speed to woods afar;*
> *For the scheme that was nursed by the Culpepper hearth*
> *With the slowly smoked cigar–*
> *The scheme that smouldered through winter long*
> *Now bursts into act-into war–*
> *The resolute scheme of a heart as calm*
> *As the Cyclone's core.*
>
> Herman Melville–description of Grant on the eve of the Wilderness in *Battle-Pieces*, 1866

The proximity of The Wilderness and Chancellorsville battlefields enables you the opportunity to explore two of the Civil War's most important sites in a single day. If you choose the longer ride you can ride the Jackson Trail West, where Stonewall Jackson led his troops on their famous flanking march. By continuing through the Wilderness and riding a short distance to the Wilderness Exhibit Shelter, you can hike the Gordon Flank Trail. Returning to the Chancellorsville Battlefield, you can hike the Hazel Grove-Fairview Trail or the Chancellorsville History Trail. Any combination of rides or hikes will give you a full day of learning and outdoor recreation.

Directions:

0.0 Exit Visitor Center to right on Bullock Road.
Please visit the center and get any supplemental literature for rides and hikes. The Stonewall Jackson Monument in front of the center marks the approximate location of Jackson's wounding by his own men on the evening of May 2, 1863. In the dark, Jackson had ridden down the Bullock Road to check Union positions. Returning to their own lines, Jackson and his small scouting party were mistaken for Union cavalry. The 18th North Carolina opened fire injuring many members of the party, including Jackson who was shot three times.

Stonewall Jackson's 26,000 troops used this trail through the woods at Chancellorsville for the Civil War's most daring flanking march.

0.8 Stop. Right on Route 610 (Ely's Ford Road).
Overwhelmed by the Confederate charge on their right flank on the afternoon and evening of May 2 and the continued pressing of the attack on the morning of May 3, the Union was forced to retreat toward the Rappahannock. The Union commander, Joseph Hooker, ordered defensive positions built to enable the crossing. The apex of these entrenchments was directly across the road at this intersection.

1.5 Stop. Continue straight across intersection with Route 3 (Orange Turnpike). Use caution. This is the Orange Plank Road.
Chancellorsville was not a town, but rather a crossroads where the Chancellors had built an imposing brick farmhouse that also served as an inn for travelers. Around this structure there was a 100-acre clearing. The combination of the clearing and intersection of roads made it the center of fighting on May 2–3.
Standing on the porch of the house, Union General Joseph Hooker was hit on the head by part of a column splintered by a Confederate shell. Dazed and partially parylyzed he rode to the rear without leaving clear commands for his subordinates.

2.6 Continue straight at intersection with Furnace Road.
Lee and Jackson met here on the night of May 1 to plan Jackson's flanking march. You are now leaving the Fredericksburg-Spotsylvania National Military Park.

3.4 Stop. Right on Route 612 (Catharpin Road).
Jackson's supply train paralleled his flanking march by using this road. At 7.4 Miles there is a small store on the left. This is the only store on the ride.

7.6 Stop. Right on Brock Road.
Todd's Tavern was located across Brock Road at this intersection. During the Battle of the Wilderness Confederate and Union cavalry clashed at this spot. After the clash, the Union cavalry under Sheridan camped by the road just south of here. Their encampment blocked the Union infantry on their way to Spotsylvania along Brock Road. Grant was forced to sleep at this site because of the bottleneck of troops heading south.

Directions: Jackson Trail West-Wilderness Spur.

8.8 Left on Jackson Trail West. If you choose the shorter ride, continue straight on Brock Road and skip to directions for Jackson Trail East.
This dirt road is the same one Jackson used to flank the Federals on May 2. The lead elements of his column, more than ten miles in length, reached this point at about 1 p.m. Rather than march north on the Brock Road Jackson had his troops continue through the woods on this little used farm trail. At 9.9 Miles you cross Poplar Run Stream. Use caution.

10.2 Right at Hill Top Farm Lane, still on Jackson Trail West.

11.1 Stop. Left on Brock Road.

12.3 Stop. Left on Route 621 (Orange Plank Road).
From this point Jackson's men headed north spreading out on both sides of the Orange Turnpike. They launched their attack on the Union right flank starting about 5 p.m.

You are now entering The Wilderness Battlefield. On the morning of May 5, 1864 the Confederate III Corps, under A.P. Hill, marched east on the Orange Plank Road. At 11:30 a.m. they encountered a Union division and a fierce fight developed for control of this intersection. Both armies sent in reinforcements, but their effectiveness was hampered by the narrow roads and thick woods.

Fighting continued through the day and resumed on May 6. The Union maintained control of the intersection and was able to push the Confederates west along the Orange Plank Road, but was unable to achieve a victory.

13.0 Right on Hill-Ewell Drive.
This road follows the general direction of the battle lines drawn by both sides on May 5–6, during the Battle of The Wilderness. The heavy second growth forest made any concerted troop movements very difficult and neither side was able to unite their flanks. Confederate trenches are still visible on your right. At 15.7 Miles there is a picnic area and a restroom.

16.4 Stop. Intersection with Route 20 (Orange Turnpike).
The Widerness Exhibit Shelter is 0.1 Mile to the right on Route 20. Use caution if you decide to ride to it. Traffic can be heavy on Route 20 and there is no shoulder. The Gordon Flank Attack Trail starts at the shelter.

The Orange Turnpike was the focus of the second major action of the Battle of the Wilderness. The Confederate II Corps faced the Union VI and V Corps on both sides of this road. Neither side made much progress for the two days, until the Confederates, under General Gordon, made a flank attack. It was successful until cut short by darkness on May 6. Except for sporadic skirmishing between pickets, this ended the Battle of the Wilderness.

16.4 Turn around at intersection and retrace route to intersection of Jackson Trail West and Brock Road.

24.0 Stop. Left on Brock Road.

9.1 (24.3) Right on Jackson Trail East.
This dirt road is the same one Jackson used to flank the Federals on May 2, 1863. You are heading in the opposite direction from their march. You are in the Chancellorsville part of the park. Look for the remains of the railroad which was still unfinished during the war. The 23rd Georgia used the cut as a defensive position after being driven back from Catherine Furnace.

11.9 (27.1) Bear left on Sickles Drive (paved).
The Federal III Corps, commanded by Major General Daniel Sickles, had seen Jackson's men marching across their front and attacked with two divisions. They decimated the 23rd Georgia which had been posted as a flank guard by Jackson. However, they in turn were stopped by Confederate artillery and an attack on their left flank by A.P. Hill's men. After the fight Sickles became convinced the Confederate movement was a retreat to the southwest and Jackson was permitted to continue the rest of his march unmolested. The remains of Catherine Furnace are visible on your left.

12.7 (27.9) Bear left on Stuart Drive.
After the conclusion of Jackson's flanking march and attack on the evening of May 2, the two halves of the Confederate army were separated. Jeb Stuart, who replaced the wounded Jackson, realized that in order to facilitate a reunification the Confederates would have to seize this hill, known as Hazel Grove. Before dawn on May 3, the Union artillery, under orders from Joseph Hooker, withdrew from the hill. The Confederates were able to seize it after encountering only minor resistance.

From this height the Confederates could bombard the Federals, who were reforming closer to Chancellorsville. The two wings of Confederate infantry succeeded in reuniting about a half mile in front of this spot. This insured a complete Confederate victory and made a Union retreat a neccessity. The Hazel Grove-Fairview Hike starts here.

13.6 (28.8) Stop. Straight across Route 3 (Orange Turnpike). Use caution.

13.7 (28.9) Right into parking at Visitor Center.

End of tour.

Start:
Spotsylvania, Spotsylvania County, Virginia; I-95 to Exit 118
(Route 606 West). Right on Route 208 to Spotsylvania. Straight
through traffic light in Spotsylvania. Right at entrance to
Fredericksburg and Spotsylvania Military Park. Parking is on
the left at the exhibit shelter.

Ride(s):
6.4 or 34.2 Miles; Flat with a few small hills.

Hike(s):
1.5 and 7 Miles. The Laurel Hill and Spotsylvania History Trails
(incorporates the Laurel Hill Trail) connect some of the most
important Spotsylvania Battlefield sites. The trails are blazed
and well maintained. Detailed maps are available at the
Chancellorsville Visitor Center and the Spotsylvania Exhibit
Shelter.

Reading:
Grant and Lee: The Virginia Campaigns 1864-1865, William A.
Frassanito, (Scribner's, New York, 1983)

After the Battle of the Wilderness on May 5–6, 1864, Lee tried to
figure out Grant's next move. Through the heavy smoke that
enveloped the battlefield on May 7, Confederate scouts saw
Grant's ambulance train heading northeast. Casualties had been
heavy on both sides and Lee thought that maybe Grant would
follow the ambulances with his army and regroup at
Fredericksburg.

However, later in the day Lee received reports of Federal cavalry to the southeast, near Spotsylvania Court House. When he
received reports of Federal artillery being moved in that direction, he became convinced that Grant was planning to keep
pressing south toward Richmond. Spotsylvania Court House, a
small crossroads, was the logical place to block this movement.
Lee gave orders to General Richard Anderson (replacing the
injured James Longstreet) to prepare two divisions to march
south that night.

Once again, Lee had correctly deduced his Union counter-

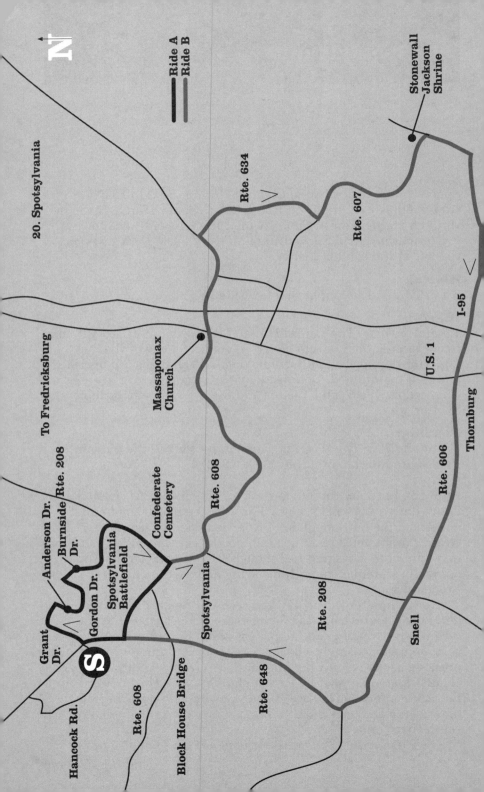

N

Ride A
Ride B

20. Spotsylvania

To Fredricksburg

Stonewall
Jackson
Shrine

Rte. 634

Rte. 607

I-95

U.S. 1

Thornburg

Massaponax
Church

Anderson Dr.

Burnside Rte. 208
Dr.

Confederate
Cemetery

Rte. 608

Rte. 606

Grant
Dr.

Gordon Dr.

Spotsylvania
Battlefield

S

Spotsylvania

Rte. 208

Snell

Hancock Rd.

Rte. 608

Block House Bridge

Rte. 648

part's intentions. By 11 p.m. both armies were underway. Although the Federals had the better route, along the Brock Road, their progress was slowed by their own cavalry who had decided to camp across the road, near Todd's Tavern. The Confederates maintained a parallel march along a track cut through the woods (Lee had ordered the track cut a few days earlier when he foresaw the possibility of such a movement).

> Our men would reach over the logs and fire into the faces of the enemy, would stab over with their bayonets; many were shot and stabbed through the crevices and holes between the logs; men mounted works and with muskets rapidly handed them kept up a continuous fire until they were shot down, when others would take their places and continue the deadly work.
>
> General Lewis A. Grant, U.S.A., May 12, 1864

This foresight combined with the Federal's confusion at Todd's Tavern gave the Confederates the edge. When, on the morning of May 8, the first Federal division reached the Alsop Farm, north of Spotsylvania Court House, they encountered Anderson's infantry blocking their way. A fierce skirmish developed and the Battle of Spotsylvania was underway. The Confederates were able to entrench and by the afternoon of May 9 their defenses resembled an inverted V, with the apex facing north. This would become known as the Mule Shoe.

Grant would spend the next two weeks trying to penetrate Lee's line. Some of the Civil War's fiercest fighting took place along this concentrated battlefield. The fighting on May 12 was so heavy that mature oak trees were felled by small arms fire. This area of the heaviest fighting at the Mule Shoe's apex became known as the Bloody Angle. While the Federals were able to momentarily break Lee's line, they were repulsed and Grant would have to continue south by flanking Lee's right, rather than take the direct route to Richmond.

These rides and hikes cover the entire Spotsylvania Battlefield National Park. In addition, the longer ride explores some of the other Civil War sites in the area, including the Stonewall Jackson Shrine. Most of the surrounding countryside remains undeveloped and is ideal for bicycling.

Directions: Ride A

0.0 Exit parking to left on Grant Drive.

The battle started just west of this spot, when the Confederates blocked the Union march south on May 8. The Union entrenched along a line paralleling this road (which did not exist at the time of the battle). Their trenches are still visible. Union General John Sedgwick was killed by a sniper's bullet just south of this site on May 9.

At .6 Miles is Upton's route. On May 10, Colonel Emory Upton led an assault on the Mule Shoe from this spot. The attack was briefly successful, but could not be sustained when Upton failed to receive support.

0.9 Right on Anderson Drive.
The Bloody Angle, the Apex of the Mule Shoe, is to the east of this intersection. At dawn on May 12, Hancock's II Corps, attacked the Confederate defenses across these fields. The assault routed the Confederate defenders, who had had much of their artillery removed to counter a possible Union flanking march, and sent them moving south. Anderson Drive parallels the western curve of the Mule Shoe.

1.4 Yield. Left on Gordon Drive.
Along this line, the advancing Federals were met with a Confederate countercharge, led by General Gordon. Desperate hand to hand fighting ensued and the Federal charge was stalled. The Federals fell back to the captured Confederate entrenchments and close fighting would continue, in a pouring rainstorm, for the next eighteen hours. The Confederates, who had fought all day without rest and food, were forced to withdraw from the entrenchments during the night. They filled a new defensive position 500 yards south of this road. The dirt road on the left leads to the McCoull House Ruins.

2.1 Right on Burnside Drive.
In conjunction with Hancock's assault on the Mule Shoe Apex, General Ambrose Burnside launched an attack on the Mule Shoe's eastern curve at this spot. Burnside's forces were also met with a countercharge, and after losing 1,200 men were forced to fall back. The road on the left leads to the East Angle site. The Union assault on the apex first struck this spot. Over 2,500 Confederates were taken prisoner.

3.2 Stop. Right on Route 208. Use caution, moderate traffic.
On May 19 the Confederate II Corps marched northeast in search of the Federal right and the possibility of intercepting their supply line. They encountered the newly arrived Federal heavy artillery. These raw troops had been pulled from the defenses around Washington and formed into an infantry force. Most were facing fire for the first time, but they performed well and stopped the Confederate advance. The fighting occured just

west of the modern intersection of Route 208 and Route 628. This was the last major engagement of the Battle of Spotsylvania. The Spotsylvania Confederate Cemetery is located across this road, as you enter town.

4.4 Traffic light. Right on Brock Road.
This is Spotsylvania Court House. The control of this crossroads was the goal of both armies, after The Wilderness. Cavalry from both armies skirmished in town before the main infantry battle. Historic Spotsylvania Court House and the Spotsylvania County Museum are at this intersection.

6.3 Right on Grant Drive. Sign for Fredericksburg-Spotsylvania Military Park.

6.4 Exhibit shelter and parking on left. End of tour.

Directions: Ride B

(Follow directions for Ride A to 4.4 Miles).

4.4 Traffic light. Left on Route 208.

5.0 Left on Route 608 (Massaponax Church Road).
After Stonewall Jackson was wounded at Chancellorsville, his

The Stonewall Jackson Shrine at Guinea Station, Virginia.

left arm was amputated by his personal physician, Dr. Hunter McGuire. Robert E. Lee feared that he might be captured while he rested near Wilderness Tavern, so he ordered Dr. McGuire to accompany Jackson to Guinea Station. This rail station was located twenty-four miles southeast, safely behind Confederate lines.

McGuire prepared an ambulance and on the morning of May 4, Jackson started to Guinea Station. This ride follows part of this route.

8.8 Right, still on Route 608.
While these roads are now well-paved, they were very rough during Jackson's journey. His aide and cartographer, Jedekiah Hotchkiss, rode ahead of the ambulance to choose the best route. He directed a small force of laborers to remove obstructions and fill in holes to ease Jackson's pain. The road was full of walking wounded and supply wagons, who had to be ordered to clear the way. Often Hotchkiss was cursed and his orders were ignored until the men learned that the wounded Jackson was following. Then these hardened soldiers and mule drivers would remove their hats and cheer Jackson.

9.9 Traffic light. Straight across Route 1 intersection.
Massapanox Church is on the left at this intersection. This church was the site of a council of war on May 21, 1864. Grant and Meade and their staffs sat in church pews in the front yard and discussed the Union army's next move after Spotsylvania. Photographer Timothy O'Sullivan took a famous series of photographs of this meeting. Jackson's ambulance turned right at this intersection.

11.8 Right on Route 634 (Flippo Road).

14.4 Left on Route 607 (Guinea Station Road).
You are again following the route of Jackson's ambulance.

15.0 Right, still on Route 607 (Route 660 straight-dirt).

17.1 Stop. Left on Route 607-606 (Stonewall Jackson Road).

17.2 Left on dirt drive (sign for Stonewall Jackson Shrine). House is at the end of the drive.
Jackson arrived here at night on May 8. The ride had been hard on Jackson and he was suffering from nausea. He was supposed to be placed in the Chandler's main farm house, but there were other wounded already there, so Mcguire had him placed in the adjacent small low frame building.

Jackson would spend the last days of his life in this building.

At first, he appeared to be recovering from his injury and subsequent amputation. However, soon complications developed and Jackson's condition worsened. At 3:30 p.m. on May 10, Jackson died. His last words were, "Let us cross over the river and rest under the shade of the trees."

The Stonewall Jackson Shrine is open Saturday–Monday, 9 a.m.–4 p.m. It is the property of the National Park Service. The house has been restored to its 1863 appearance and contains many period pieces, including Jackson's bed and the Chandler clock. An excellent lecture concerning Jackson's final days is given; there is a small bookstore.

17.8 Exit property to right on Route 606, continue straight over railroad tracks, continuing on Route 606.
The Guinea Station railroad depot was located here. This station was an important depot for the Confederates during the battles of Fredericksburg, Chancellorsville, The Wilderness and Spotsylvania. After Spotsylvania it was seized by the Union and held for the rest of the war.

23.0 Traffic light. Straight across Route 1, still on Route 606.
Parts of both armies marched south along Route 1, after Spotsylvania. Lee formed his next defensive line south of the North Anna River, fifteen miles south of this intersection.

27.5 Stop. Straight, now on Route 208-606.

29.9 Right on Route 648 (Blockhouse Road).

32.8 Stop. Straight across Route 608 (Robert E. Lee Highway).
The Confederate III Corps marched along this road to Spotsylvania on May 9. The Block House Bridge, an important Po River crossing, was located just west of this intersection. On May 10, the Union right occupied this area, but withdrew to establish new lines north of Spotsylvania. This road reenters the National Park.

34.0 Stop. Left on Route 613 (Brock Road).

34.2 Right on Grant Drive, sign for Fredericksburg-Spotsylvania Military Park.

34.3 Parking on left.

End of tour.

21 Williamsburg-Yorktown

Start:
Williamsburg, Williamsburg County, Virginia; I-95 to I-295 East.
Take Exit 200, I-64 East to Exit 238 (Route 143 South) to
Williamsburg. Stay to the right and follow Route 132 to the
Colonial Williamsburg Visitor Center.

Ride(s):
31.9 Miles; Rolling hills.

Hike(s):
Walking tour of Williamsburg. While the main focus of the
Williamsburg historic area is the Colonial period, some of the
buildings and living-history demonstrations have Civil War and
19th-century relevance. Detailed maps are available at the
Visitor Center and shuttle buses leave for the historic area every
few minutes. General admission tickets for all exhibition buildings are available at the Visitor Center.

Reading:
To the Gates of Richmond: The Peninsula Campaign, Stephen W.
Sears, (Ticknor & Fields, New York, 1992)

It was no coincidence that Jefferson Davis was inaugurated on
George Washington's Birthday and delivered his inaugaral
address at the foot of Washington's statue in downtown
Richmond. Occurring just eighty years after the American
Revolution, the Civil War was in part a struggle over the ideals
of this earlier war. Soldiers and politicians on both sides sought
justification for their actions in the deeds and words of this earlier generation. In 1862, this ideological struggle became an
armed struggle at some of the very places where these principles
were formed and made possible—Yorktown and Williamsburg.
  On March 17, 1862 one of the largest waterborne military
expeditions in history began. George McClellan decided to move
most of the Union army to Fort Monroe (which the Union army
still held), on the tip of the Virginia peninsula, sixty miles southeast of Richmond. During the next three weeks hundreds of
ships would transport over 100,000 men and their equipment to
Fort Monroe from Washington. From Fort Monroe, McClellan

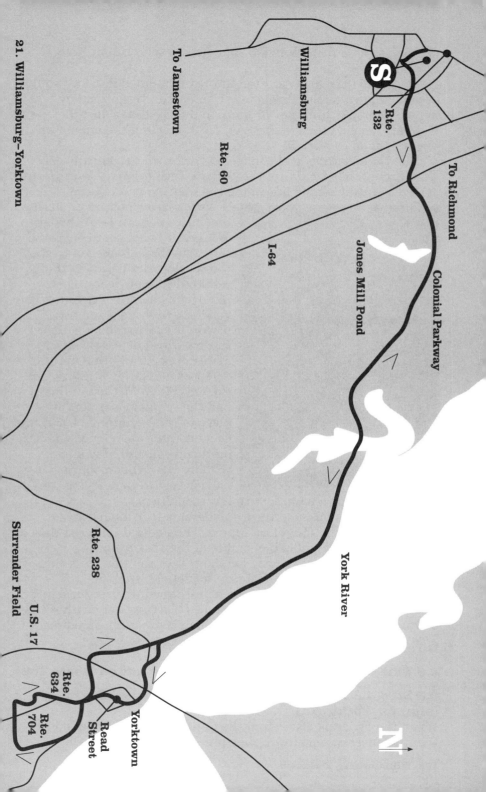

21. Williamsburg–Yorktown

Williamsburg

Rte. 132

To Jamestown

Rte. 60

I-64

To Richmond

Colonial Parkway

Jones Mill Pond

York River

Rte. 238

Surrender Field

U.S. 17

Rte. 634

Rte. 704

Read Street

Yorktown

S

N

planned to assault Richmond, supported by the Union Navy on the James and York rivers.

On April 4 the army started toward Richmond in what would become known as the Peninsular Campaign. Despite many impediments, including poor maps and torrential rains, the Federals reached the outskirts of Yorktown, and the enemy, on the afternoon of April 5.

The Confederates had connected Yorktown entrenchments (reinforcing the remains of the British Revolutionary War defenses), with a twelve-mile line along the western bank of the Warwick River, southwest across the entire peninsula. Although McClellan had a six to one superiority in force, he began to show the caution and paranoia that would ultimately lead to his removal as head of the army. The Federal army spent the next month preparing to lay siege to the Yorktown defenses, although ample opportunity to flank the defenses along the Warwick line existed. When McClellan finally had the requisite artillery in place at the beginning of May, the Confederates abandoned the line on the evening of May 3 and withdrew to Williamsburg. They had succeeded in delaying the Federal army for a month, with few casualties.

> *Fellow citizens, on this, the birthday of a man most identified with the establishment of American independence,.we have assembled to usher into existence the permanent Government of the Confederate States. Through the instrumentality, under the favor of Divine Providence, we hope to perpetuate the Principles of our Revolutionary Fathers. The day, the memory, and the purpose seem fitly associated.*
>
> Jefferson Davis, Inaugural Address, February 22,1862

The Federals pursued the Confederates to Williamsburg, where a battle was fought on May 5. The Federals entered the old Colonial capital the next day and held the area from Williamsburg to Fort Monroe for the rest of the war. This ride connects part of the Williamsburg Battlefield with the Confederate and Union positions at Yorktown. Except for a few miles through Yorktown, the ride takes place entirely within the Colonial National Historical Park which is great for bicycling.

Directions:

0.0 Exit Williamsburg Visitor Center to left on Route 132.

0.3 Stop. Left on Colonial National Historical Parkway (sign for Yorktown).
When the Federals discovered the Confederates had abandoned their defenses at Yorktown, they pursued with cavalry. On the

The Colonial National Parkway at Jones Mill Pond. The woods in the background was the scene of fighting during the Battle of Williamsburg.

afternoon of May 4, they caught up with the Confederates and skirmishing occurred east of Williamsburg (modern-day Route 60). The Confederates then withdrew to a series of forts and entrenchments east of town. Confederate General James Longstreet had been ordered by the head of the army, Joseph Johnston, to delay the Federal pursuit until the Confederate wagon train was safely on the way toward Richmond. On May 5, enough Federal infantry had arrived to engage the Confederates and the Battle of Williamsburg started at 7:30 a.m.

The battle unfolded in three separate actions. Southeast of Williamsburg, Joseph Hooker's division engaged Confederates under James Longstreet. The Confederates succeeded in driving the Federals from their defenses and captured a number of field pieces. By 3 p.m. Federal reinforcements, under Philip Kearny, reached the field and drove the Confederates back to their original line. The battle in this area continued for the rest of the day, with no clear victor. The remains of the largest Confederate defensive position, Fort Magruder, are still visible on the property of the Fort Magruder Inn and Conference Center on Route 60.

Meanwhile, the third action developed northeast of town. Federal General Winfield Scott Hancock had been ordered to lead 2,500 men north and occupy undefended Confederate redoubts on a ridge. The Colonial Parkway crosses this ridge at 3.2 Miles. Hancock siezed the ridge and the earthworks without any opposition. At this point, the Federals were behind the main Confederate line and could cut off their retreat. However, Longstreet had become aware of Hancock's presence and ordered Jubal Early and D.H. Hill to attack with 2,700 men.

These Confederates, who were resting in reserve at the College of William and Mary, marched in this direction and charged the Federals through the woods without properly scouting their exact position or strength. Hancock saw the approaching Confederates and withdrew to the cover of the ridge's eastern slope. When the Confederates got within range, Hancock's men stood and delivered a devastating volley. The Confederate attack stalled and Hancock then made the order to charge. This bold order would secure Hancock's reputation and earn him the title, Hancock the Superb. The Battle of Williamsburg ended with 2,239 Federal casualties and 1,603 Confederates dead, wounded or missing. The Federals entered Williamsburg the next day, when the Confederates withdrew toward Richmond.

At 3.7 Miles is Jones Mill Pond. The Federal's flanking march took place through the woods east of the pond and across the Cub Creek Dam (modern Colonial Parkway). There is a historical marker at the pond. Continuing on the Colonial Parkway, there are more historical markers and picnic areas. At 6.2 Miles the road crosses Felgate's Creek and the York River is now on the left. There is a picnic area at Ringfield.

11.4 Left at sign for Yorktown Victory Center (just before Route 238 overpass).

11.7 Stop. Left on Route 238 (Water Street).
Entrance for the Yorktown Victory Center is on the right. The Yorktown Victory Center is operated by the Commonwealth of Virginia and has various displays pertaining to the Colonial period. Admission is charged.

Continue down hill, follow road to right along the York River. The land on the opposite shore of the York River (at the terminus of the Route 17 bridge) is Gloucester Point. This was the location of another Confederate fort. It was abandoned when the Confederates withdrew from Yorktown. Union gunboats controlled this section of the York River for the remainder of the war.

12.4 Right on Read Street (one way). Shift to low gear as you go up hill and enter historic Yorktown.

12.6 Stop. Continue straight across Main Street, still on Read Street.

There are many restored, reconstructed and original 18th century structures in the Main Street area. Yorktown was occupied by both armies during the war and many buildings were destroyed when a Union powder magazine exploded in the old courthouse. The house located cater-cornered from this intersection (on the corner with Nelson Street) is the Nelson House. Built in 1711 it was the home of Thomas Nelson Jr., signer of the Declaration of Independence. During the Civil War it served as a hospital for both armies. Tours are given by the National Park Service.

12.8 Stop. Left on Ballard Street.

13.1 Left at sign for Yorktown Battlefield Visitor Center.
The Visitor Center has many displays and programs pertaining to the Colonial period and Yorktown in the Civil War. Detailed maps of the battlefield are available.

The earthworks in the vicinity of the Visitor Center (designated the British line) are, in fact, the Confederate earthworks from 1862. The Confederates enlarged and altered the works in preparation for the Union siege. The Confederate commander, General John Magruder, used slaves from plantations on the peninsula for most of this construction.

13.5 Exit Visitor Center to left on Park Road.

14.2 Right on Park Road (one way), opposite Redoubts 9 and 10.
This road enters the location of the Federal siege line (Heintzelman's corps occupied this flank). Advance lines of pickets and sharpshooters from both armies fought in these woods during the month-long siege.

14.9 Stop. Right on Park Road, over Wormley Creek Dam.
The Federals had great difficulty in bringing their huge siege artillery through this swampy area.

15.9 Stop. Continue straight across Cook Road.

16.0 Stop. Right on Park Road.

16.1 Right on Park Road (The entrance to Surrender Field is on the left).
Turning left at this point leads to the nine-mile encampment tour. A bike path at Washington's Headquarters leads to the five-mile Newport News Park bike path. Union trenches and Dam No. 1, an important defensive position, are visible at this park.

16.6 Stop. Right on Surrender Road (Route 634).

17.1 Stop. Left on Route 704.
Confederate forces, under D.H. Hill, occupied the fields to the left of this road. The Yorktown National Cemetery is on this road; 2,200 Union dead from the Peninsular Campaign are buried here.

17.5 Stop. Left on Park Road (Route 238).

17.7 Left on Colonial Parkway (sign for Williamsburg and Jamestown).

30.3 Right on Route 132 (sign for Williamsburg Visitor Center).

30.6 Right at Visitor Center entrance.

End of tour.

22 Malvern Hill-Glendale

Start:
Richmond National Battlefield Park (Malvern Hill Unit),
Henrico County, Virginia; I-95 South to I-295 South. Exit 22,
Route 5 East (New Market Road) to National Park sign at Route
156. Bear left at Carters Mill Road to entrance on left.

Ride(s):
5.9 Miles; Flat with a few small hills.

Hike(s):
No hikes included in this section.

Reading:
*Gone For A Soldier: The Civil War Memoirs of Private Alfred
Bellard*, Edited by David Herbert Donald, (Little, Brown and
Company, Boston, 1975)

After seizing Williamsburg on May 5, 1862 McClellan's Army of
the Potomac continued its slow progress toward Richmond.
Because of McClellan's habitual caution, which earned him the
nickname the "Virginia Creeper," the army didn't reach the outskirts of Richmond
until May 24. On May
31 the Confederates
attacked the Federals
at Fair Oaks (the
Battle of Seven Pines),
just east of Richmond.
The attack did not go
as planned. As the
Confederate comman-
der, General Joseph E.
Johnston, rode to the
front to observe his
army's progress, he

> The Spires of Richmond, late beheld
> Through rifts in musket-haze,
> Were closed from view in clouds of dust
> On leaf-walled ways,
> Where streamed our wagons in caravan;
> And the Seven Nights and Days
> Of march and fast, retreat and fight,
> Pinched our grimed faces to ghastly plight-
> Does the elm wood
> Recall the haggard beards of blood
>
> Herman Melville, Malvern Hill, 1866

was severely wounded. The battle ended indecisively the following day, with General Gustavas Smith in charge of the
Confederate army.

Because Smith proved he was not qualified for leadership of

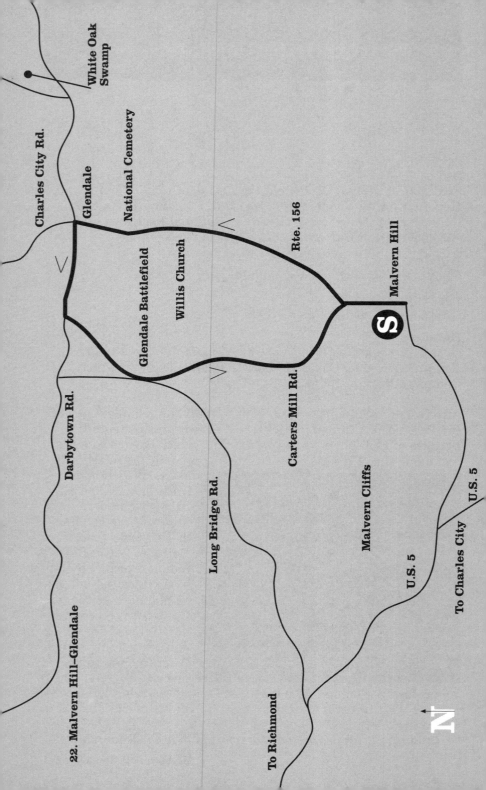

22. Malvern Hill–Glendale

White Oak Swamp

Charles City Rd.

Glendale

National Cemetery

Glendale Battlefield

Willis Church

Rte. 156

Malvern Hill

S

Darbytown Rd.

Long Bridge Rd.

Carters Mill Rd.

Malvern Cliffs

U.S. 5

U.S. 5

To Charles City

To Richmond

N

the army (he would resign from the army a few days later), Jefferson Davis found himself in need of a commander at a very critical time. He made his decision quickly; Robert E. Lee would assume overall command of the Confederate army in Virginia.

After Seven Pines, the Confederates were still backed against Richmond, with the Union Army of the Potomac entrenching close enough to lay siege to the capital. After reorganizing the Confederate army, Lee decided to continue the offensive. He called for Stonewall Jackson's army to leave the Shenandoah Valley and join the campaign.

From June 25 to July 1 the two armies fought in a campaign that would become known as the Seven Days Battles. This campaign, which includes the battles of Oak Grove (June 25), Mechanicsville (June 26), Gaines's Mill (June 27), Savage's Station (June 29), Glendale (June 30), and Malvern Hill (July 1), succeeded in driving the Federals from Richmond, despite the fact that Lee was unable to score a decisive victory. In fact, the Union ended the campaign with a decisive victory at Malvern Hill, when their artillery and infantry took advantage of a commanding defensive position and decimated the attacking Confederate infantry. However, after this decisive victory, the ever cautious McClellan withdrew south to Harrison's Landing and the Peninsula Campaign came to an end.

This short ride connects the Malvern Hill Battlefield with the Glendale Battlefield. There are many interpretive markers and landmarks, including the Glendale National Cemetery and the Willis Church. Although only a few minutes from Richmond, the landscape has changed little since the war. There is an exhibit shelter with an audio station and map at Malvern Hill. Public restrooms and picnic facilities are located at Fort Harrison (seven miles west on Route 5).

Directions:

0.0 Exit exhibit shelter area to left on Route 156 (Willis Church Road).
Even before the start of the Seven Days Battles, McClellan had considered the withdrawal of the Army of the Potomac's base of operations to Harrison's Landing on the north bank of the James River, which offered the protection of Union navy gunboats. After the Union defeat at Gaines Mill, McClellan became convinced of the necessity of the withdrawal and informed his corps commanders.

They fought a fighting retreat for the next three days and the entire army reached Malvern Hill on the evening of June 30. Although the plateau is less than 100 feet higher than the surrounding countryside, it was an excellent defensive position. The

Glendale National Cemetery.

Confederates would have to coordinate their attack in a swampy and wooded area and then charge up the gradual rise, across open fields. Federal infantry were deployed on the lower slopes and artillery crowned the ridge, with reserves deployed south toward River Road (modern Route 5).

0.3 Bear right, still on Willis Church Road.

Lee had been frustrated during the previous week by his subordinates' inability to follow orders and coordinate their attacks on the retreating Army of the Potomac. Now that the Federals had almost reached the safety of the James River, a sense of desperation gripped Lee.

Despite the warning of General D.H. Hill not to attack such a strong position, Lee was committed to one more battle. He deployed his infantry in a mile long arc, facing south, with the center near this intersection. Around noon on July 1, the Confederates came under heavy bombardment from the Federal artillery on the hill. Two Union gunboats, the *Mahaska* and *Galena*, participated in the bombardment later in the day, from their location in the James River.

Although the Confederate artillery responded and caused

some damage, it was unable to soften the Federal position for an infantry charge. However, because of confusion concerning Lee's orders and miscommunication among the various infantry commanders, the infantry attack was launched around 4 p.m. While some Confederates would get within a few dozen yards of Federal artillery, the Federal line held. The Confederates suffered 5,355 casualties causing D.H. Hill to write later, "It was not war, it was murder."

As you continue north on Willis Church Road, there are a few historical markers, describing various aspects of the battle and the Confederate approach. As you start up the small hill after crossing Western Run, you enter the area of the Glendale (Frayser's Farm) Battlefield.

1.8 Willis Church on left and Glendale National Cemetery on right.

On June 30 General Lee and the Confederate army had an excellent chance to split the Union army in two and, perhaps, even destroy it at the Battle of Glendale. In full retreat, the Union army was stretched from White Oak Swamp to near Malvern Hill, a distance of over five miles. Their progress south was hampered by their supply wagons, ambulances and walking wounded. The Union commander, General McClellan, spent the day of battle on a navy gunboat (having a fine dinner) and failed to leave battle orders or delegate an overall field commander.

Stonewall Jackson's army pursued the Federal rearguard at White Oak Swamp, while most of Lee's command marched east in two separate columns along the Charles City and Darbytown roads toward the small crossroads of Glendale, the logical attack point. An additional force of 6,000 men, under General Theophilus Holmes, marched northeast from Drewry's Bluff to face the Federals who had already reached Malvern Hill. In all, Lee expected over 70,000 Confederates, in four separate columns, to simultaneously attack the Federals on both flanks and the center.

The various Federal corps commanders were aware of the Confederate pursuit and, despite little coordination among their forces, took defensive action. They formed their lines, facing west, in the fields and woods approximately 200 yards to the west (left) of this road (known as the Quaker Road during the war). The line ran from a half mile south of Willis Church to a mile north (along the Charles City Road).

The Willis Church was used as a Confederate hospital after the battles of Glendale and Malvern Hill. The Glendale National cemetery was dedicated after the war and is the final resting place of American soldiers from four wars.

2.5 Stop. Left on Darbytown Road.

This small crossroads is Glendale. Two miles to the northeast, along modern Route 156, Stonewall Jackson's attack on the Union rearguard at the White Oak Swamp Bridge stalled. Historians have debated the cause of Jackson's poor performance during the Seven Days Battles and at Glendale. Most evidence seems to support sheer physical exhaustion as the reason for Jackson's actions (or more correctly, inaction). When Jackson's 23,000 troops reached the White Oak Swamp, they found the only bridge in the area burned. The Swamp in the immmediate area prohibited the infantry from crossing and the Federal artillery commanded a small rise on the opposite side. An artillery duel started, but Jackson failed to send infantry across at two fords his scouts discovered. Jackson spent the afternoon sleeping and the Federals were able to shift troops from this area to the main engagement at this location.

The second Confederate column, under General Benjamin Huger, advanced toward Glendale along the Charles City Road from the northwest. Their progress was slowed by Federals wielding axes, felling trees in front of the road. When Huger's men finally chopped their way through the abatis, they faced Slocum's division, one mile northwest of this intersection. Huger, like Jackson, was content to engage in a meaningless artillery duel and never ordered his infantry to attack.

3.1 Left on Long Bridge Road.

The main Confederate force, divisions under James Longstreet and A.P. Hill, marched east on Darbytown Road, south to Long Bridge Road, and then northeast toward Glendale. When the Confederate's fourth column, Holmes's men, collapsed under artillery fire from the Federals at Malvern Hill, Lee became aware that the only infantry attack at Glendale would come from Longstreet's and Hill's divisions. At about 5 p.m. he ordered the advance.

The battle took place in the fields north and south of this intersection, where the Confederates encountered the initial Federal defensive line. The fields (the Nelson or Frayser Farm) and woods to the left as you continue southwest on Long Bridge Road were the location of some of the war's most intense hand to hand fighting. The Confederates succeeded in briefly breaking the Federal line, but Federal reinforcements and darkness prevented them from sustaining the advantage. The Federal army was not cut in two and during the night they continued their march south to Malvern Hill. Robert E. Lee was furious at his subordinates failure to coordinate the attack and commented the next morning, "Yes, he will get away because I cannot have my orders carried out!"

4.0 Yield. Left, still on Long Bridge Road.

4.2 Left on Carters Mill Road.
This was the location of the Confederate right at Glendale. As you continue south on Carters Mill Road, you reenter the Malvern Hill Battlefield. Confederate troops occupied the fields (the Carter Farm) on both sides of the road, awaiting orders for their ill-fated infantry charge. These fields occupied a small rise which the Confederates planned to use as an artillery location. However, a large majority of these guns could not reach the location. Those that did came under tremendous fire from the Federal artillery on Malvern Hill and were largely disabled. A similar artillery plan on the Confederate left (one mile to the east) also failed and the plan to enfilade the Federal position collapsed.

5.6 Stop. Right on Willis Church Road.
As you continue up the small rise, the field to the right was the location of the heaviest Confederate casualties during the Battle of Malvern Hill. On the morning of July 2, Union Colonel William Averell looked down these slopes from his position at the top and observed, "A third of them were dead or dying, but enough were alive and moving to give to the field a singular crawling effect."

5.9 Right at entrance to Malvern Hill exhibit shelter.

End of tour.

23 Fort Harrison

Start:
Richmond National Battlefield Park (Fort Harrison Unit),
Henrico County, Virginia; I-95 South to I-295 South. Exit 22,
Route 5 West (New Market Road) to National Park entrance on
the left. Parking is at the Fort Harrison Visitor Center on the
left side of Battlefield Park Road.

Ride(s):
10.0 Miles; Flat.

Hike(s):
Short walking tours of Fort Harrison and Fort Brady. Tours are
self-guiding with interpretive markers.

Reading:
The Negro in the Civil War, Benjamin Quarles, (Boston, 1953)

On June 2, 1864 Grant gave orders for an attack on the
Confederate army entrenched northeast of Richmond at Cold
Harbor. The attack, launched on the morning of June 3, was a
disaster. After the attack Grant
commented to his staff, "I
regret this assault more than
any one I ever ordered." Grant,
who had shown more patience
than any previous Union commander, had now had enough of
the slow flanking of Lee's army.
From the Wilderness to Cold
Harbor both armies had suffered over 80,000 casualties and
Grant was now ready for a bold-
er movement.

> Once let the black man get upon
> his person the brass letters U.S.,
> let him get an eagle on his but-
> tons and a musket on his shoul-
> der and bullets in his pocket,
> and there is no power on earth
> which can deny that he has
> earned the right to citizenship
> in the United States.
>
> Frederick Douglass,
> August 1863

On the night of June 12 Grant
ordered the Army of the Potomac to withdraw from Cold Harbor
and move south. His goal was Petersburg and the important
supply lines that fanned out from the city. It was a bold move.
The army would have to cross the Chickahominy and the James

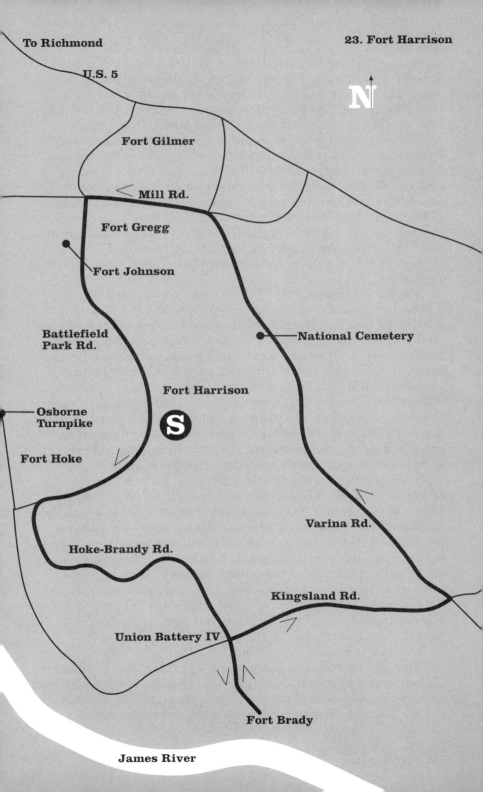

23. Fort Harrison

To Richmond

U.S. 5

N

Fort Gilmer

Mill Rd.

Fort Gregg

Fort Johnson

Battlefield
Park Rd.

National Cemetery

Fort Harrison

Osborne
Turnpike

S

Fort Hoke

Varina Rd.

Hoke-Brandy Rd.

Kingsland Rd.

Union Battery IV

Fort Brady

James River

rivers without Lee's knowledge. If Lee discovered the movement, he could strike Grant's army while it was divided by one or both of the rivers. The crossing of the James presented the most difficult engineering problem of the entire war. Here, Grant's engineers had to build a pontoon bridge 2,100 feet long over the James at a point where it was over 100 feet deep.

The movement was successful, but when the vanguard of Grant's army reached the undermanned Confederate defenses around Petersburg, their attack stalled. Lee finally became aware of Grant's surprise move and rushed reinforcements to Petersburg and southeastern Richmond. The long awaited siege of Richmond and Petersburg was underway. For the next ten months the armies faced each other across closely constructed siege lines. The Union periodically attempted to find a weakness in the Confederate defenses and drive Lee from Richmond and Petersburg.

Among the troops used in these actions were all black regiments; by the end of the siege the Army of the Potomac would contain 38 black regiments. While some Union commanders had doubts about the formation and use of black regiments, their performance in this campaign dispelled most of these officers' cynicism and prejudice. During the war, over 180,000 blacks served in the Union army and navy. They were paid less than their white counterparts, were largely denied promotion above the rank of sergeant and suffered higher casualty rates. Despite these obstacles, black regiments performed as well as any in the army and by the end of the war, twenty three black soldiers were honored with the Congressional Medal of Honor.

Black troops performed with particular gallantry in the attack on New Market Heights and Fort Harrison (Chaffin's Farm) on September 29, 1864. In another attempt to break the Richmond and Petersburg defenses, Grant approved General Benjamin Butler's plan to advance north and west from Deep Bottom and Aiken's Landing and attack the Confederate defenses. An important part of this attack force was a division of U.S. Colored Troops from XVIII Corps. The Federals surprised the Confederates and after heavy losses succeeded in capturing New Market Heights and Fort Harrison, but were unsuccessful in driving the Confederates from the rest of their defenses.

This ride connects the various forts that were established in the area before and after the assault. Fort Harrison National Cemetery is also included on this ride. The ride is easy with very little traffic and is ideal for the casual bicyclist. The Visitor Center has a small display, a picnic area and restrooms.

Directions:

0.0 Exit Visitor Center to left on Battlefield Park Road.
Fort Harrison is located to the east of (behind) the Visitor
Center. This fort, which had walls up to 27 feet high and 15 feet
thick, was the largest in this section of Richmond's defenses.
The Union assault on Fort Harrison started early in the morn-
ing of September 29. Twenty-five hundred Union troops swept
across the fields to the east of the fort. They faced only 800 inex-
perienced, poorly equipped Confederate artillerymen.
Confederate reinforcements, veteran troops under General
Gregg, arrived too late to stop the Union assault.

The Union was in control of the fort by 7 a.m., as the
Confederates withdrew to other elements of their defensive line.
However, because of heavy casualties, exhaustion and ineffective
leadership, the Union was unable to sustain the attack and
break through to Richmond.

On September 30, Lee and many Confederate reinforcements
crossed the Chaffin's Bluff bridge and prepared to retake Fort
Harrison. More than 9,000 Confederates massed to the south-
west of the fort and the attack was launched in the afternoon.
However, this assault failed because of poor coordination by
Lee's subordinates. The Union held the fort (renamed Fort
Burnham) for the rest of the war.

1.1 Left on Hoke-Brady Road.
Fort Hoke was located just west (right) of this intersection. The
Federals succeeded in capturing this fort for a short time on the
morning of September 29. The small Federal force was driven
back by the reformed Confederate line and the presence of two
Confederate ironclads, the *Fredericksburg* and *Richmond*, which
hurled huge shells at the attacking Federals from the James
River. Fort Hoke would remain in Confederate hands until the
abandonment of Richmond in April 1865. There are Union
entrenchments, visible to the right, along this road.

3.0 Stop. Continue straight across Kingsland Road.
More trenches are visible. Union Battery IV was located at this
intersection.

**3.9 Stop at end of road, Fort Brady walking trail. After
tour of Fort Brady return to intersection with Kingland
Road.**
Park bicycle next to sign. This short trail leads to the remains of
Union Fort Brady. This fort anchored the left of the new Union
siege line after the capture of Fort Harrison. The 1st
Connecticut Heavy Artillery occupied the fort from October
1864 to April 1865. They engaged in duels with Confederate

Fort Harrison National Cemetery.

artillery on Chaffin's Bluff and with Confederate ironclads in the James River.

4.8 Stop. Right on Kingsland Road.
This historic road was used by both armies during the war.

5.6 Left on Varina Road.
On the night of September 28, part of Edward Ord's XVIII Corps crossed the James River on a pontoon bridge three miles south of this intersection at Aiken's Landing. They marched north on Varina Road to assault Fort Harrison.

7.0 Fort Harrison National Cemetery on left.
The Federal assault on Fort Harrison took place through the fields on both sides of the cemetery. Fort Harrison is located 100 yards southwest of the cemetery. As the Federals marched across these fields, they faced artillery fire from the Confederate defenders.

8.1 Left on Mill Road.
After capturing New Market Heights (4 miles east), Federals under General William Birney, marched west on New Market

Road (Route 5) and Mill Road. Just west of Varina Road they encountered stiff Confederate opposition at Fort Gregg and Fort Gilmer. Black troops, the 5th, 7th, and 9th United States Colored Troops, were at the forefront of the assaults. Despite having the numerical superiority, the Federal assaults were unsuccessful. Casualties were very high. Only one man of the 189 in the 7th that assaulted Fort Gilmer returned to safety.

8.7 Stop. Left on Battlefield Park Road.
Fort Gilmer was located .2 Mile north of this intersection. Fort Gregg was located just to the left of the intersection. There are interpretive markers at the remains of both forts. Fort Johnson was located at 9.4 Miles on the right. The Confederates successfully defended this fort from Federal assault. After Fort Harrison was captured, new lines were built connecting Fort Johnson with Fort Hoke to the southwest. Trenches are visible on both sides of the road.

10.0 Left at Fort Harrison Visitor Center.

End of tour.

Start:
Petersburg, Petersburg County, Virginia; I-295 South to Exit 9,
Route 36 West. Turn right at Petersburg National Military Park
Visitor Center sign. Parking is adjacent to Visitor Center.
Admission is charged.

Ride(s):
6.4 Miles; Flat with a few small hills.

Hike(s):
Fort Stedman and Crater hiking trails. Each trail is about one
mile and starting points are located adjacent to the road.

Reading:
The Army of the Potomac: A Stillness at Appomattox, Bruce
Catton, (Doubleday & Company, Garden City, N.Y., 1953)

When the Army of the Potomac's vanguard, 18,000 men of the
XVIII Corps, reached the eastern outskirts of Petersburg at 7
a.m. on June 15, 1864, their success seemed assured. Most of the
Confederate army remained
entrenched north and east of
Richmond, thirty miles away.
Petersburg was strongly fortified, but the commander of the
city's defenses, General Pierre
Beauregard, had only 2,200
troops to man the four miles of
forts east of Petersburg. But, once again, caution and poor judgment affected the Union command.

> *The last hour of the
> Confederacy has arrived.*
>
> General Pierre Beauregard
> in a message to Robert E. Lee,
> June 17, 1864

The attack did not start until 7 p.m. that evening and
although the Federals overwhelmed part of the Confederate line,
they stopped their attack after a few hours. The Confederates
were able to entrench one mile behind their original line and
prepare for the next Union assault. The Federals repeatedly
attacked during the next three days, but despite overwhelming
superiority were unable to break the Confederate line.
    Meanwhile, Lee finally became convinced that Grant had

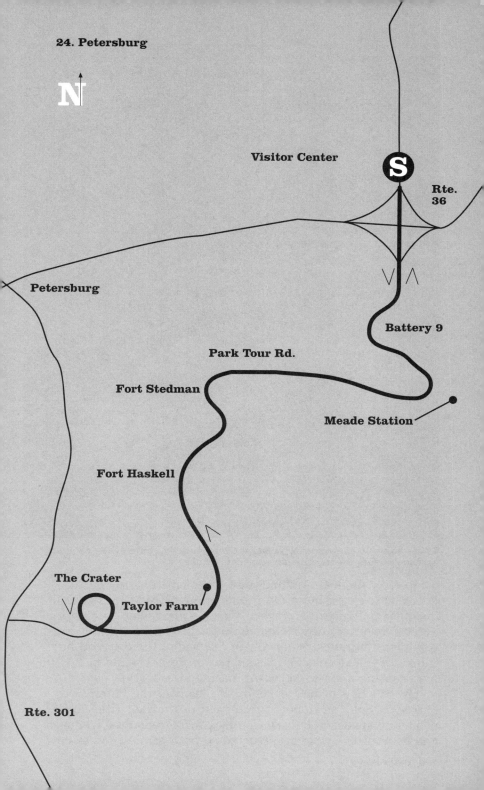

24. Petersburg

N

Visitor Center

S

Rte. 36

Petersburg

Battery 9

Park Tour Rd.

Fort Stedman

Meade Station

Fort Haskell

The Crater

Taylor Farm

Rte. 301

These sharpened stakes (a fraise) were an integral part of the complex entrenchments during the siege of Petersburg.

completely flanked him and moved the entire Army of the Potomac to Petersburg. On the morning of June 18, Lee and most of the Army of Northern Virginia arrived at Petersburg. Veterans poured into the trenches to the cheers of their over-whelmed comrades. When Grant learned of their arrival he called off the attacks and issued new orders. He had lost 11,000 men gaining a few miles of inconsequential terrain.

Grant's new orders were for the Army of the Potomac to entrench. Soldiers in both armies put down their rifles and picked up spades and axes. Complex forts, redoubts, trenches and bombproofs were constructed by both armies, sometimes only a few hundred feet from each other. As the summer progressed the Union army slowly circled Petersburg to the south, while at the same time probing the Confederate line for any weaknesses. The Confederate line thinned and supplies became scarcer as the Union extended their siege line and seized control of roads and rail lines.

However, the Confederate line held through the summer and fall, despite such bold Union attacks as the Battle of the Crater. Winter brought calm to the siege, but both armies realized spring would bring a new offensive to the campaign. Grant started pushing further west in February. By March he was ready for a major offensive, one he hoped would end the war in Virginia. On April 1, the Federals defeated George Pickett's division at Five Forks and completed their encirclement of Petersburg. The next day, Grant launched the final assault on Petersburg, a concentrated bombardment and infantry charge that succeeded in driving the Confederates from Petersburg and Richmond.

This short ride in Petersburg National Military Park follows the Confederate and Union entrenchments east of Petersburg. Included are Union encampment sites, earthworks and the remains of Fort Stedman and The Crater. This is one of the best National Military parks for bicycling and hiking with miles of trails designated specifically for these activities.

Directions:

0.0 Exit Visitor Center parking past entrance kiosk over bridge.
Part of the final Union siege line was located just to the east and north of the parking lot. There is a short walking path to the location of the Dictator, a 17,000 pound Union siege mortar. The Visitor Center has displays, a map program and a bookstore.

0.1 Right on Park Tour Road (one way). The left lane is specifically designated for bicycling and walking. Use caution. Watch for other bicyclists, pedestrians, and parked cars. You will use this road for the entire tour.
Union entrenchments were located to the left. Some earthworks are still visible.

0.5 Battery 8 on left.
This Confederate battery, was captured by black troops during the initial Union attack.

0.8 Battery 9 on left.
This Confederate battery was also siezed by black troops on June 15, 1864. The Union IX Corps camped in the area. A trail

Fort Stedman was the location of the Army of Northern Virginia's last offensive on March 25, 1865.

leads to Meade Station, an important point on the City Point and Army Railroad. This railroad was built to bring supplies to the Union army from the James River. The railroad was completed in September 1864 and the subsequent delivery of fresh food and new supplies helped to improve the morale of the beleagured Federals.

1.4 Harrison Creek on right.
Beauregard's troops fell back to this point after the original Union attack on June 15. They held this line for two days and then withdrew closer to Petersburg.

1.7 Fort Stedman on right.
This area was the location of some of Petersburg's heaviest fighting on two dates. On June 18, 1864 the 1st Maine Heavy Artillery Regiment, fighting as an infantry unit, was decimated as it attacked Confederate positions west of this spot. Of the 900 men in the regiment, 632 were dead, wounded or missing after the attack—the greatest Union regimental loss of the war.

In February 1865, Lee realized that Grant would soon launch an offensive to take Petersburg. In desperation, he decided to launch an attack and ordered General John Gordon to devise a plan. Three weeks later, Gordon reported to Lee his complex plan to attack Fort Stedman. Fort Stedman was strongly defended, but only 150 yards from the Confederate line at Colquitt's Salient. Gordon's plan called for Confederate axemen to chop

This reconstructed opening marks the location of the Crater tunnel entrance.

through the abatis in front of the fort. They would be followed by small detachments, each with a specific Union redoubt as their goal. Once these redoubts and Fort Stedman were in Confederate hands, four divisions of Confederates would fill the gap and attack the Union line north and south of this point.

The attack was launched at 4 a.m. on March 25. The initial phase went according to plan and the surprised Federals in Fort Stedman were taken prisoner or forced to retreat. But the Confederates could not gain much ground beyond the fort and soon the Federals in other parts of the line counterattacked. By 8 a.m. it became clear that the Confederate attack would fail and they were driven back to Fort Stedman. The attack cost the Confederates 3,500 casualties and prisoners. This defeat was the last offensive action by the Army of Northern Virginia in the Civil War.

There is a walking trail connecting Fort Stedman with Colquitt's Salient and the 1st Maine Monument. There are interpretive markers with audio narration. No bikes are allowed on the trail. There is a bicycle rack located near the start of the trail.

2.1 Fort Haskell on right.
This Union fort was used to stop the Confederate attack on Fort Stedman.

2.7 Taylor Farm site on right.
Heavy fighting occurred on the Taylor Farm during the intitial

Union attack on June 15–18, 1864. The Confederates fell back across the farm and established new lines west of here. During the Battle of the Crater, many of the Union's 160 artillery pieces fired from this ridge.

3.2 Stay to right on circle to Crater Walking Trail starting point.

The Battle of the Crater was one of the most bizarre and tragic episodes of the Civil War. On June 18, 1864 the 48th Pennsylvania established its lines within 130 yards of the Confederates, closer than any other Federal unit. This unit, made up largely of coal miners, dug a 510-foot tunnel under the Confederate line and planted 8,000 pounds of black powder directly under a Confederate fort known as Elliot's Salient.

The explosives were detonated at 4:40 a.m. on July 30 and when the cloud of smoke and dirt settled the Union troops rushed across the open ground to find a crater 200 feet long, fifty feet wide, and up to 30 feet deep where the Confederate fort previously stood. Almost 300 Confederates had been killed by the tremendous explosion and those still alive were too shocked to respond to the attack. However, the crater and the complex tunnels and defensive lines beyond it confused and delayed the Union attack. Soon, other Confederate units were rushing into the area and many Union troops became trapped in the crater, where the Confederate troops poured their fire from the surrounding walls.

The Crater became a death trap for many Federals, including dozens of black troops who were killed by the Confederates despite surrendering. Grant called it "the saddest affair I have witnessed in the war." Over 3,000 Federal troops were killed, wounded, or taken prisoner. After the battle the Confederates established new lines closer to the Federals.

The Crater walking tour leads to the tunnel entrance and along the tunnel to the Crater. It is self-guiding with interpretive markers and monuments.

3.2 Continue around circle and return to Park Road to the left. The bicycle lane is on the right.

6.4 Visitor Center parking.

End of tour.

25 Sayler's Creek

Start:
Sailor's Creek Battlefield Historical State Park (Virginia has changed the spelling of the State Park to Sailor's; the historical spelling of the battlefield and creeks is Sayler's), Amelia County, Virginia; I-95 South to Richmond. Take Exit 187 to Route 64 West. Take immediate Exit 186 to I-195 South, to Route 76 (Powhite Parkway). Exit on Route 288 to Route 360 West (sign for Amelia and Farmville). Right on Route 307. Right on Route 617 to parking at Sailor's Creek Battlefield at the Hillsman House on the right.

Ride(s):
14.4 Miles; Hilly.

Hike(s):
No hikes in this section.

Reading:
An End to Valor: The Last Days of the Civil War, Philip Van Doren Stern, (Houghton Mifflin, Boston, 1958)

Driven from Petersburg and Richmond, Lee's army began a desperate march southwest with the hope of reaching North Carolina and joining forces with General Joseph E. Johnston's army. The various elements of the army converged on Amelia Court House, which had been chosen as a rendezvous in case of a Union breakthrough. Lee's contingency plan had called for supplies and rations to be stockpiled at Amelia Court House for his starving troops. But when the troops arrived on April 4, they found that the food had never been sent from Richmond. They spent most of the following twenty hours foraging in the surrounding countryside, but their effort produced little food.

> *My God! Has the army been dissolved?*
>
> General Robert E. Lee,
> Sayler's Creek, April 6, 1865

The Union cavalry were just hours behind the Confederates and soon started harassing wagon trains and capturing strag-

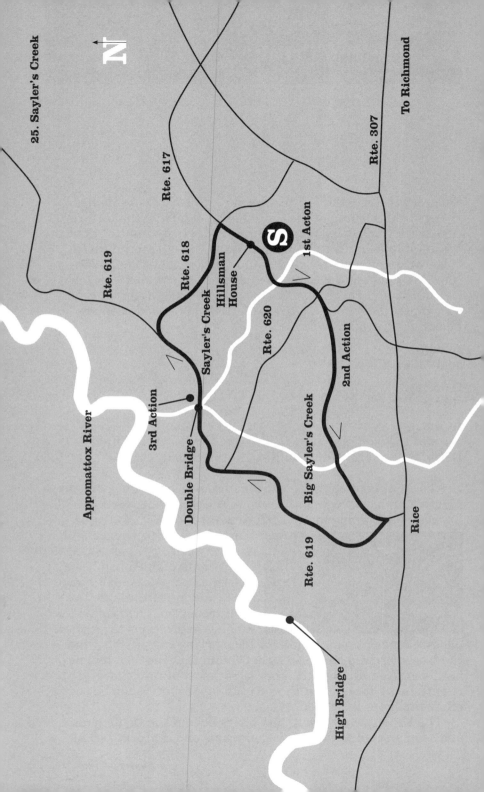

25. Sayler's Creek

N

To Richmond

Rte. 307

Rte. 617

Rte. 619

Rte. 618

1st Action

S

Hillsman House

Sayler's Creek

Rte. 620

2nd Action

Appomattox River

3rd Action

Double Bridge

Big Sayler's Creek

Rice

Rte. 619

High Bridge

glers, thousands of whom were too exhausted, hungry and demoralized to continue the march. Those that could continue, headed west toward Farmville, on the Southside Railroad where Lee hoped to get food shipped from Lynchburg. By now, Federal infantry were also beginning to approach the Confederates and blocked any possible march south.

Lee and his commanders realized their race was becoming more and more desperate and forced their troops to march all afternoon on April 5 and continue, without rest, through the night. The column lengthened as commanders found it impossible to maintain order and soldiers fell out to forage and fall asleep by the roadside. The Federals were just as ardent in their pursuit; men who had served for four years would recall it as their hardest march of the entire war.

On the morning of April 6, Lee's army was spread from Rice's Station to Amelia Springs with Longstreet's command in the front, followed by corps under Anderson and Ewell. Gordon's corps acted as rear guard. Federal cavalry and infantry repeatedly struck the rear and left flank of the Confederate column. These repeated attacks and an increasing lack of cohesion between the Confederate corps created gaps in their line of march. Finally, the Federals attacked with a total of 35,000 troops on the afternoon of April 6 in three separate actions around Big and Little Sayler's Creeks. All three actions were a disaster for the Confederates and they lost over 7,000 men, one fourth of Lee's total army.

The remainder of the Confederate army struggled through Rice's Station and onto Farmville, where they finally received rations. As they started to cook them, the Federals arrived and they were forced to retreat again, this time toward Appomattox. At Appomattox Court House, the Confederates reached the end of their final journey and on April 9, Grant received Lee's formal surrender.

This ride retraces part of Lee's retreat and the Federal pursuit. It connects the three actions of the Battle of Sayler's Creek, the last major battle of the Civil War in Virginia. There is very little traffic in this rural area and the battlefield (state and private property) is well-preserved. The state has installed radio transmitters with audio loop narration at four sites, so you might want to carry a radio tuned to 1620 AM on your ride. The closest public restrooms and stores are located in Farmville, four miles west on Route 460.

Directions:

0.0 Exit Hillsman House to left (south) on Route 617.
This was the Union position, occupied by Wright's VI Corps with 10,000 men, during the middle action at Sayler's Creek. They placed their five batteries of artillery on this ridge and shortly after 5 p.m. bombarded the Confederates, 3,000 men under Richard Ewell, positioned on the ridge to the southwest.

The house was used as a hospital after the battle. There are interpretive markers, a battle painting, radio narration and an excellent view toward the Confederate position on the property.

At 0.4 Miles the road crosses Little Sayler's Creek. After the terrific bombardment (the Confederates had no artillery to respond with), the Federals deployed in the fields behind the Hillsman House and prepared to attack. They marched down the hill and crossed the creek and swampy ground with great difficulty. They started to come under fire as they started up the ridge held by the Confederates.

At 0.8 Mile there is an interpretive marker on the left and the Sayler's Creek Battlefield Memorial on the right. This was Ewell's defensive position. As the Federals marched up the ridge, the Confederates held their fire until they were within 100 yards. Their initial volley stopped the Federal charge, and they countercharged into the Federal center. However the Federals continued their charge on both flanks and soon overwhelmed the Confederates. Two thousand Confederates were captured, including Generals Ewell and George Washington Lee (Robert E. Lee's eldest son).

1.3 Stop. Continue straight across Route 620, still on Route 617.
This is the area of the southern battle action. When General Anderson's 6,000 troops became separated from Longstreet's lead corps. Federal cavalry, under General Wesley Merritt, rode into the gap and blocked their march at this crossroads.

Anderson's troops dug shallow earthworks and prepared for a cavalry charge. They repulsed the initial attack, but when

The Union occupied this ridge overlooking Little Sayler's Creek on the afternoon of April 6, 1865.

George Custer's division charged the center of the Confederate line and horses leaped the earthworks, it was too much and the line broke. About 3,000 of Anderson's men were captured, while the remainder fled through the woods to the right.

1.5 Right on Route 600.
Those Confederates that escaped emerged from the woods along this road and succeeded in reaching Lee and Longstreet at Farmville. At 4.0 Miles the road crosses Big Sayler's Creek.

5.3 Stop. Right on Route 619.
At 7.4 Miles is a historical marker describing the small battle at High Bridge, which is located one mile west of this spot (trespassing laws are strictly enforced). When Lee and Longstreet reached Rice's Station they learned that the Federals had dispatched 900 men to destroy this railroad bridge and an adjoining wagon bridge, important avenues of retreat. Longstreet ordered 1,200 Confederate cavalry troopers, under Thomas Rosser, to pursue and stop the Federals at all costs.

The Confederates caught the Federals at the bridges and a fierce cavalry battle soon developed. The Confederates won the battle, saved the bridges and took more than 800 prisoners. However, when the Confederates crossed the bridges after their defeat at Sayler's Creek, they failed to completely destroy the wagon bridge and the Federals were able to pursue without much delay.

10.1 Double Bridge and the confluence of Little and Big Sayler's Creeks.

This is the area of the third action at the Battle of Sayler's Creek. A few miles east of this spot at Holt's Corner, Gordon's rearguard became separated from Ewell's troops when they mistakenly followed the Confederate wagon train, which had veered north to avoid capture. The wagon train and Gordon's men were bogged down by the narrow bridges (one of which collapsed) at this point. The final phase of the battle took place as Gordon's men were driven into this valley by Federals from Humphrey's II Corps. There is an interpretive marker and radio transmitter describing the action.

Shift gears as you start up the steep hill to the Lockett's farm area. As the sun began to set on April 6, Gordon realized that the jam at Double Bridge would prevent the wagon train from crossing the creeks and escaping, so he drew his troops into a defensive position on this ridge and awaited attack. Humphrey's 15,000 troops soon drove the few thousand Confederates off the ridge and into the valley. The desperate stand there, among the wagons, was unsuccessful and Gordon lost 1,700 men, 70 ambulances and 200 wagons. Among the items found in the wagons were millions of dollars of Confederate money. That night, Union soldiers played high-stakes poker around their campfires with the worthless money.

11.5 Right on Route 618.

This is the Route of Gordon's retreat and Humphrey's pursuit.

13.5 Stop. Right on Route 617.

This is Holt's Corner,which was the location of a skirmish and the point of separation of Gordon from the other Confederates. There is a monument to W.R. Turner, a historian who was responsible for researching much of Lee's retreat route.

14.4 Hillsman House on left.

End of tour.

Calendar

The following annual events have a Civil War or 19th-century theme. Event dates often vary, so please call to confirm. This is a partial listing, contact local and state tourist centers for other events.

January
Stonewall Jackson's House, Lexington, VA. Stonewall Jackson's Birthday Celebration. 703-463-2552

February
Sully Plantation, Chantilly, VA. Black History Celebration. 703-437-1794

Colvin Run Mill, Great Falls, VA. Civil War Reenactment. Features the 54th Massachusetts, who were the subject of the movie *Glory*. 703-759-5241

Museum of the Confederacy, Richmond, VA. Black History Celebration with living history demonstrations. 804-649-1861

March
Waynesboro, VA. Civil War Reenactment, Battle of Waynesboro. 703-949-8072

Jamestown, VA. Military Through the Ages. Live military demonstrations of all periods, including the Civil War. 804-229-1607

Belle Grove Plantation, Middletown, VA. Traditional Crafts Show. 703-869-2028

April
Kemper Mansion Grounds, Madison, VA. Civil War Reenactment and Encampment. 703-948-4382

Museum of American Frontier Culture, Staunton, VA. Spring
Farm Tour. Visit historic farms with costumed guides explaining
19th-century customs. 703-332-7850

Winchester, VA. Shenandoah Apple Blossom Festival.
Festival features traditional crafts, food and entertainment.
703-662-3863

Surratt House, Clinton, MD. John Wilkes Booth Escape Bus
Tour. Day-long event retraces Booth's route. Reservations
required. 301-868-1121

Surratt House, Clinton, MD. Civil War Encampment.
301-868-1121

Charles Town, Martinsburg, Harpers Ferry and Shepherdstown,
WV. Historic House and Garden Tour. Many important Civil War
buildings are featured in this tour. 304-535-2627

May
Virginia Military Institute, Lexington, VA. New Market Day
Observance. Parade ground ceremony honoring cadets who
fought at the Battle of New Market. 703-464-7207

New Market Battlefield Historical Park, New Market, VA. Civil
War Reenactment of Battle of New Market. 703-464-7207

Sully Plantation, Chantilly, VA. Reenactment of Skirmish
Between Mosby's Men and Federal Cavalry. 703-437-1794

John Lee Pratt Park, Fredericksburg, VA. Civil War
Reenactment. 703-373-7909

Confederate and National Cemeteries, Fredericksburg, VA.
Memorial Day Ceremonies. Color guard, speakers and wreath
laying honoring Civil War dead. 703-373-6122

Stonewall Cemetery, Winchester, VA. Confederate Memorial
Service. Program honors 3,000 Confederate dead interred here.
703-662-1937

Shenandoah University, Winchester, VA. Civil War Institute.
Program features lectures by noted Civil War authorities and
trips to Civil War sites. 703-665-4588

Culpeper, VA. Culpeper Day. Downtown festival featuring crafts,
food and history. 703-825-8628

Gainsboro, VA. North-South Skirmish Spring Nationals
Program. Civil War weapons firing and demonstrations.
703-888-7917

Yorktown, VA. Civil War Weekend. Encampment and living history demonstrations. 804-898-3400

Jonathan Hager House, Hagerstown, MD. Civil War Living History Demonstration. 301-739-8393

Grantsville, MD. National Pike Festival. Festival from Washington County west to Ohio along Pike (Route 40). Features local foods, crafts and living history demonstrations. 301-895-3315

South Mountain Fairgrounds, Arendtsville, PA. Apple Blossom Festival. Country festival featuring food, music and crafts. 717-334-6274

Gettysburg, PA. Memorial Day Parade. Parade through town to National Cemetery with traditional flower laying ceremony. 717-334-6274

June

Fredericksburg, VA. Market Square Fair. Festival featuring food, entertainment, traditional crafts and living history demonstrations. 703-371-4504

Oak Ridge Farm, Arrington, VA. Civil War Reenactment. 804-263-4168

Belle Grove Plantation, Middletown, VA. Shenandoah Valley Farm Craft Days. Traditional craft demonstrations and sales. 703-869-2028

Point Lookout State Park, Scotland, MD. Confederate Days. Artillery and rifle demonstrations with walking tours of old Confederate prison site. 301-872-5688

Rockville, MD. Yesteryear 1861. Civil War Reenactment and Festival. 301-309-3340

Harpers Ferry, WV. Mountain Heritage Arts and Crafts Festival. Artists, craftspersons, food and entertainment. 304-725-2655

Philippi, WV. Blue and Gray Reunion Festival. Civil War reenactment, encampment and Civil War Ball. 304-457-3700

Lewisburg, WV. Civil War Reenactment. 304-645-1000

Gettysburg College, Gettysburg, PA. Civil War Institute. Lectures and tours are given by prominent Civil War scholars. 717-337-6590

July

Town Park, Funkstown, MD. Civil War Reenactment and Festival. 301-797-0948

Antietam National Battlefield, Sharpsburg, MD. Maryland Symphomy at Antietam. Concert, fireworks and cannon fire on 4th of July. 301-797-4000

Monocacy National Battlefield, Frederick, MD. Battle Anniversary and Reenactment. 301-662-3515

Fort Frederick State Park, Big Pool, MD. Military Field Days. Military encampments and demonstrations from all eras, including the Civil War. 301-842-2155

Cumberland, MD. Chesapeake and Ohio Canal Boat Festival. Living history demonstrations, canal boat tours, music, crafts and canal history lectures. 301-729-3136

Carroll County Farm Museum, Westminster, MD. Old-fashioned Fourth of July. Old fashioned games, crafts, and entertainment, followed by fireworks at dusk. 410-876-2667

Gettysburg, PA. Gettysburg Civil War Heritage Days. Features a lecture series, encampment and battle reenactment. 717-334-6274

August

Robert E. Lee House, Alexandria, VA. Civil War Living History Day. 703-548-8454

Manassas, VA. Prince William County Fair. Traditional crafts, demonstrations and food. 703-368-0173

Yorktown, VA. Celebrate Yorktown. City-wide festival. 804-890-3324

Union Mills Homestead, Union Mills, MD. Corn Roast Festival. 410-848-2288

Greenbrier State Forest, White Sulphur Springs, WV. Battle of Dry Creek Reenactment. 304-536-4373

September

Williamsburg, VA. Publick Times. 18th and 19th-century festival with food, crafts and entertainment. 800-447-8679

Winchester, VA. International Street Festival. 703-665-0079

Jonathan Hager House, Hagerstown, MD. Civil War Reenactment. 301-739-8393

Boonsboro, MD. Boonsboro Days. Traditional crafts, food and entertainment. 301-582-6969

New Market, MD. New Market Days. Antiques, crafts and living history demonstrations. 301-831-6791

Poolesville, MD. Civil War Encampment. Signal Corps demonstration, food, parade and crafts. 301-428-8927

Antietam National Battlefield, Sharpsburg, MD. Battle Anniversary. Special events and tours. 301-432-5124

Surratt House, Clinton, MD. John Wilkes Booth Escape Bus Tour. Day-long event retraces Booth's route. Reservations required. 301-868-1121

Weston, VA. Stonewall Jackson Heritage Arts and Crafts Jubilee. Arts, crafts, Civil War reenactments and encampments. 304-269-1863

October
Manassas, VA. Fall Jubilee. Traditional festival in old town Manassas. 703-361-6599

Appomattox, VA. Historic Appomattox Railroad Festival. 804-352-2338

Falmouth, VA. Historic Falmouth Walking Tour. Visit many historic sites associated with Battle of Fredericksburg. 703-888-7917

Cedar Creek Battlefield, Middletown, VA. Living History Weekend. Civil War reenactments, encampments, and demonstrations. 703-869-2064

Emporia, VA. Civil War Reenactment of the Hicksford Raid. 804-634-9441

Frederick, MD. In The Street. Downtown festival with entertainment, food, and crafts. 301-694-1435

Middletown, MD. Middletown Heritage Weekend. Civil War reenactment and festival. 301-371-6171

Carroll County Farm Museum, Westminster, MD. Fall Harvest Days. Agricultural festival. 410-848-7775

Brunswick, MD. Brunswick Railroad Days. Railroad museum displays, food, train rides on historic train line. 301-834-7100

Point Lookout State Park, Scotland, MD. Ghost Walk and Halloween Tour of old Civil War prison site. 301-872-5688

Guyandotte, WV. Civil War Reenactment. 304-696-5954

Harpers Ferry, WV. Living History 1860s. Revisit the political scene of the 1860s and participate in the presidential election. 304-535-6029

Arendtsville, PA. National Apple Harvest Festival. Old time festival featuring entertainment, music, crafts and orchard tours. 717-334-6274

November
Gettysburg, PA. Gettysburg Address Anniversary. Memorial service at National Cemetery. 717-334-6274

December
Stonewall Jackson's Headquarters, Winchester, VA. A Confederate Christmas. Costumed guides and traditional refreshments. 703-662-1937

Hopewell, VA. A Civil War Christmas at Hopewell. A traditional celebration at 1864 City Point National Historic Site. 804-458-9504

Fredericksburg, VA. Anniversary Ceremony of Battle of Fredericksburg. Color guard, wreath laying and speakers at Kirkland Memorial. 703-373-6122

Antietam National Battlefield, Sharpsburg, MD. Memorial Illumination. 23,110 illuminaries displayed on battlefield.

Associations

Civil War

The following is a list of local, state, and national organizations dedicated to the acquisition and preservation of Civil War property in the Mid-Atlantic Region.

The Association for the Preservation of Civil War Sites
613 Caroline Street, Suite B
Fredericksburg, VA 22401
703-371-1860

The Association for the Preservation of Virginia Antiquities
2301 East Grace Street
Richmond, VA 23223
804-648-1889

The Brandy Station Foundation
P.O. Box 165
Brandy Station, VA 22714

The Cedar Creek Battlefield Foundation, Inc.
P.O. Box 229
Middletown, VA 22645
703-869-2064

Central Maryland Heritage Trust
P.O. Box 721
Middletown, MD 21769
301-371-7090

The Civil War Trust
1225 I Street, N.W., Suite 401
Washington, D.C. 20005
202-408-5679

The Conservation Fund, Civil War Battlefield Campaign
1800 North Kent Street, Suite 1120
Arlington, VA 22209

Friends of Monocacy Battlefield, Inc.
P.O. Box 4101
Frederick, MD 21705-4101

Friends of The National Parks at Gettysburg
P.O. Box 4622
Gettysburg, PA 17325-4622

Friends of Harpers Ferry National Park
Route 3, P.O. Box 98
Harpers Ferry, WV 25425

The Lee-Jackson Foundation
P.O. Box 8121
Charlottesville, VA 22906

The Maryland Civil War Heritage Commission
Maryland Department of Transportation
P.O. Box 8755
B.W.I. Airport, MD 21240

The National Trust for Historic Preservation
1785 Mass. Ave., N.W.
Washington D.C. 20036

The Nature Conservancy
1815 North Lynn Street
Arlington, VA 22209
703-841-8781

Rich Mountain Battlefield Foundation
P.O. Box 227
Beverly, WV 26253

Save Historic Antietam Foundation
P.O. Box 550
Sharpsburg, MD 21782

The Virginia Military Institute
New Market Battlefield Historical Park
P.O. Box 1864
New Market, VA 22844
703-740-3101

Bicycling

The following is a listing of national, state, and local
organizations dedicated to bicycle recreation, education, and
advocacy. Contact your local bicycle shop for information on
other local riding clubs.

Baltimore Bicycling Club
410-792-8308

Bicycle Federation of America
1818 R Street, N.W.
Washington, D.C. 20009

Bicycling Federation of Pennsylvania
413 Appletree Road
Camp Hill, PA 17011

Bikecentennial
P.O. Box 8308
Missoula, MT 59807
406-721-1776

Frederick Pedalers Bicycle Club
P.O. Box 1293
Frederick, MD 21701

The League of American Wheelmen
6707 Whitestone Road, Suite 209
Baltimore, MD 21207
301-944-3399

Potomac Pedalers Touring Club
P.O. Box 23601
Washington, D.C. 20026
202-363-TOUR

Shenandoah Valley Bicycle Club
P.O. Box 1014
Harrisonburg, Virginia 22801

Washington Area Bicyclist Association
1015 31st Street, N.W.
Washington, D.C. 20007
202-872-9830

Williamsburg Bicycle Association
P.O. Box 713
Williamsburg, VA 23187

Winchester Wheelmen
P.O. Box 1695
Winchester, VA 22601

Bibliography

The following sources are in addition to those listed in each section. Also, the numerous brochures and maps published by the National Park Service and other organizations were of great help in writing this book.

Books

Alexander, E.P., *Military Memoirs of a Confederate* (Dayton: Morningside Bookshop, 1977)

Averell, William Woods, *Ten Years in the Saddle: The Memoir of William Woods Averell,* Ed. by Edward Eckert, (Novato, CA: Presidio Press, 1978)

Barry, Joseph, *The Strange Story of Harper's Ferry* (Shepherdstown: The Shepherdstown Register, 1984 reprint of 1904 original)

Brown, David H., *Antietam: Bloodiest Day* (Brunswick, Md.: Privately Printed, 1962)

Brown, J. Willard, *The Signal Corps, U.S.A. in the War of the Rebellion* (Boston: U.S Signal Corps Association, 1896)

Buel, Clarence and Johnson, Robert V., Editors, *Battles and Leaders of the Civil War* (New York: Century Company, 1884-1887)

Buell, Augustus, *The Cannoneer: Recollections of Service in the Army of the Potomac* (Washington: National Tribune, 1890)

Catton, Bruce, *The Coming Fury* (Garden City: Doubleday & Company, 1961)

Davis, Burke, *Jeb Stuart: The Last Cavalier* (New York: Rinehart, 1957)

Douglass, Frederick, *Life and Times of Frederick Douglass* (NewYork: Collier Books, 1962, originally published 1892)

Foote, Shelbey, *The Civil War: A Narrative* (New York: 1958-74)

Frassanito, William A., *Antietam: The Photographic Legacy of America's Bloodiest Day* (New York: Scribner's, 1978)

Frassanito, William A., *Gettysburg: A Journey in Time* (New York: Scribner's, 1975)

Freeman, Douglas Southall, *Lee's Lieutenants: A Study in Command*, 3 vols. (New York: Scribner's, 1942-44)

Goss, Warren Lee, *Recollections of a Private: A Story of the Army of the Potomac* (New York: Thomas Crowell & Co., 1890)

Hahn, Thomas F., *Towpath Guide to the Chesapeake and Ohio Canal* (Shepherdstown: American Canal Center, 1972)

Johnson, Curt and Mclaughlin, Mark, *Civil War Battles* (New York: Fairfax Press, 1977)

Krick, Robert K., *Stonewall Jackson at Cedar Mountain* (ChapelHill: University of North Carolina Press, 1990)

Long, E.B. and Long, Barbara, *The Civil War Day by Day*, (Garden City: Doubleday & Company, 1971)

Longstreet, James, *From Manassas to Appomattox: Memoirs of the Civil War in America* (Bloomington: Indiana University Press, 1960)

McClellan, H.B., *I Rode With Stuart* (Millwood, N.J.: Kraus, 1981)

McPherson, James M., *Battle Cry Freedom* (New York: Oxford University Press, 1988)

Melville, Herman, *Battle-Pieces and Aspects of the War* (New York: Harper and Brothers, 1866)

Merchant, Thomas, *History of the 84th Regiment, Pennsylvania Volunteers* (Philadelphia, 1889)

Mitchell, Reid, *Civil War Soldiers* (New York: Viking, 1988)

Myres, Frank, *The Comanches: A History of Whites Battalion* (Baltimore: Kelly Piet & Company, 1871)

Quarles, Benjamin, *Allies for Freedom: Blacks and John Brown* (New York: Oxford University, 1974)

Stiles, Robert, *Four Years under Marse Robert* (Dayton: Morningside Bookshop, 1977)

Summers, Festus P., *The Baltimore and Ohio in The Civil War* (Gettysburg: Stan Clark Military Books, 1993, originally published 1939)

Symonds, Craig L., *Gettysburg: A Battlefield Atlas* (Baltimore: Nautical and Aviation Publishing, 1992)

Tanner, Robert G., *Stonewall in the Valley: Thomas J. "Stonewall" Jackson's Shenandoah Valley Campaign, Spring, 1862* (Garden City: Doubleday, 1976)

Townsend, George Alfred, *Campaigns of a Non-Combatant* (New York: Blelock, 1982)

Von Borcke, Heros, *Memoirs of the Confederate War for Independence* (London: W. Blackwood & Son, 1866)

War of the Rebellion, Official Records of the Union and Confederate Armies, 128 vols. (Washington: U.S. Government Printing Office, 1880-1901)

Wheeler, Richard, *Sword over Richmond* (New York: Harper & Row, 1986)

Wills, Gary, *Lincoln at Gettysburg* (New York: Simon & Schuster, 1992)

Other Sources

Catton, Bruce, "Lest We Forget..." *American Heritage*,
August 1961

Cohen, Roger S., "The Civil War in the Poolesville Area"
Montgomery County Historical Society, November 1961

Frew, James, "Civil War Battles in Winchester and Frederick
County, Virginia" (Winchester: Winchester Historical Society,
1961) Pamphlet

Kimball, William J., "The Battle of Piedmont" *Civil War Times
Illustrated*, January 1967

Sword, Wiley, "Cavalry on Trial at Kelly's Ford" *Civil War
Times Illustrated*, April 1974

Wainwright, Charles S., "So Ends the Great Rebel Army..."
American Heritage, October 1962

Index

Y

York, PA, 97
York River, 166–168
Yorktown, VA, 164, 166,
168–170

Z

Zekiah Swamp, MD, 71, 73